Devon and Cornwall

Jane Chrzanowska

photography by

Jeremy Haslam & Andrew Besley

HarperCollins*Publishers*

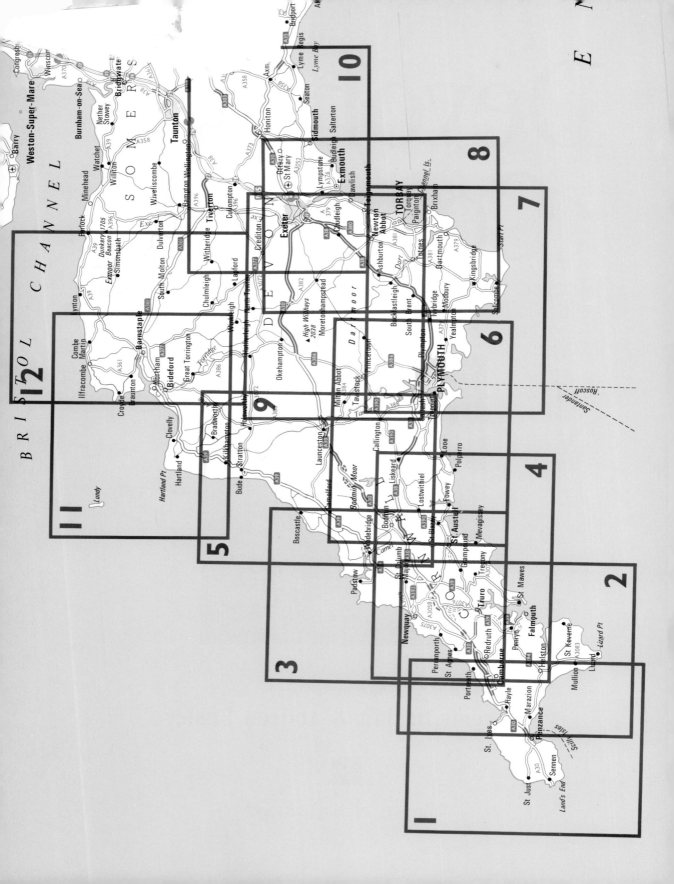

CONTENTS

Land's End

Looking west from Zennor Head (AB)

Interior of Zennor Church (AB)

Pew end, Zennor Church (AB)

Chysauster Iron-Age village (JH)

6 *Preceding page:* **Land's End** (AB)

Looking west from Tater-du (AB)

It's not difficult to see why this corner of Britain should have been the birthplace of so many myths and legends. The granite landscape is strewn with the remains of past civilizations and is the very stuff of which poetry and fables are made. At the tip of the peninsula the jagged serpentine heights and relentless Atlantic breakers are forbidding and awe-inspiring even when viewed on the brightest summer afternoon; their strength and power has been responsible for the wrecking of countless ships. The super-tanker *Torrey Canyon* is just one of the many vessels that have sunk in these treacherous coastal waters (1967).

Land's End was cultivated very early in our history. The farmers around Zennor still work on fields marked out by stone walls constructed by people of the Iron Age. Archaelogists believe that the many stone circles, quoits and dolmens (stone tables) in the area may have been early astronomical observatories, used to chart the movements of the planets.

By contrast, St Michael's Mount rises from the waves like a fairytale castle. The Mount was said to have been the home of the Cornish giant, Cormoran, and the archangel Michael allegedly appeared to a group of fishermen on the rocky south side. Originally built in the 14th century, it closely resembles its French counterpart, Mont St Michel, in Brittany. Over the years it has been used as a church, priory, fortress and private home. The Mount has been the home of several noble families over the last 400 years. It was acquired in 1660 by Sir John St Aubyn whose descendant, Lord St Leven, still lives there, although it is now owned by the National Trust.

Cornwall was a Celtic stronghold for many centuries and, like Ireland and Wales, developed its own distinctive Celtic language. A local rhyme runs 'By Tre, Pol and Pen, Ye shall know Cornishmen', and if you look at any map or in any telephone directory of the area you'll notice how many names are prefixed with these words. 'Tre' means homestead or hamlet, 'Pol' a pool or pond and 'Pen' a chief, headland or hill. As Cornwall became increasingly Anglicized, the old language gradually died out and only in the far west of Cornwall was it kept alive. The last monoglot Cornish speaker was Dolly Pentreath, a fisherwoman from Mousehole who died in 1777. Recently there has been a resurgence of interest in the old language, and it is now being taught at evening classes.

Eagle owl, Hayle Paradise Park (AB)

Penzance harbour (JH)

Trengwainton Gardens (AB)

Smuggling is, in most people's minds, inextricably linked to western Cornwall. The narrow inlets, long shallow creeks and numerous caves made the area ideal for the trade, so much so that Cornwall was for a long time the centre of British smuggling. Remote and impoverished, Cornwall was a perfect distribution point for the cargoes of wine, spirits, tobacco and bullion that reached its shores. The illegal trade reached its peak during the 18th century, when most members of the community, from street-boys to magistrates, were involved in it at some level. The most famous heroes of the smuggling fraternity were John and Harry Carter, who ran their operation from the Mount's Bay area, just up the coast from Marazion. The brothers were highly professional, and shipped their wares in a 160-ton cutter with 19 guns which travelled under cover of darkness between Penwith and Brittany. A fervent Methodist, John Carter dubbed himself 'The King of Prussia' after his idol, Frederick the Great; his favourite smuggling hideaway was called 'Prussia Cove'. Wrecking (the looting of shipwrecked vessels) was practised alongside smuggling, although it is unlikely that the stories of Cornishmen deliberately luring boats onto the rocks are true. Perhaps Parson Troutbeck of Scilly expressed the sentiments of most Cornishmen involved in the

Penberth Cove (AB)

Minack Theatre (AB)

Old school house, Marazion (JH)

Ruin near Marazion (JH)

practice when he said: 'We pray, O Lord, not that wrecks should occur, but that if they do Thou wilt drive them into the Scilly Isles for the benefit of the poor inhabitants.'

The rugged charm and beauty of the Penwith peninsula have inspired many writers and novelists. The writer Virginia Woolf spent many childhood holidays at St Ives, and her novel *To The Lighthouse* is based on an expedition to nearby Godrevy Island. D. H. Lawrence wrote much of *Women in Love* while living in a remote cottage near Zennor during World War I. The villagers were suspicious of the lights that burned late in his house and, accusing him of being a spy, forced

Chun Quoit (JH)

Fisherman with cat and lobsters, St Ives (AB)

St Ives (JH)

10   **St Ives' beach** (JH)

Granite wall (JH)

Lawrence and his German wife, Frieda, to leave. Dylan Thomas and Caitlin Macnamara moved from west Cornwall to the fishing village of Mousehole in the spring of 1938. The fishing village Llaregyb, in *Under Milk Wood*, is thought to be based on Mousehole.

This part of Cornwall also has a long association with painters, sculptors and craftsmen, who were drawn to the place because of its mild climate and exceptionally clear light. Artists' colonies were first established in Newlyn and St Ives over a century ago. The Irish painter Stanhope Forbes was the first to come. He settled in Newlyn and was later joined by Walter Langley, Frank Bramley, Norman Garston and

Rooftops, St Ives (JH)

Elizabeth Armstrong. The whole group became known as the Newlyn School. These artists took as their subjects the dramatic coastline, desolate moorland and granite landscapes, as well as the everyday life of the fishermen of Newlyn. Around the same time a group of predominantly foreign artists arrived at St Ives and set up the St Ives Art Club (1888). A second wave of artists arrived in both centres in the 1920s, including Laura Knight at Newlyn and Ben Nicholson and Christopher Wood at St Ives. Nicholson's first wife, Barbara Hepworth, set up her studio in the town in 1939 and soon afterwards the potter Bernard Leach arrived and established the Leach Pottery at Higher Stennack. A new generation of artists came to St Ives in the 1960s, many of them painters of abstract works; they included Terry Frost, Patrick Heron and Roger Hilton.

In recent years the greatest influence on Land's End has been the businessman and keen yachtsman Peter de Savary. He is the man behind many of the current initiatives for promoting the area, including Land's End Theme Park.

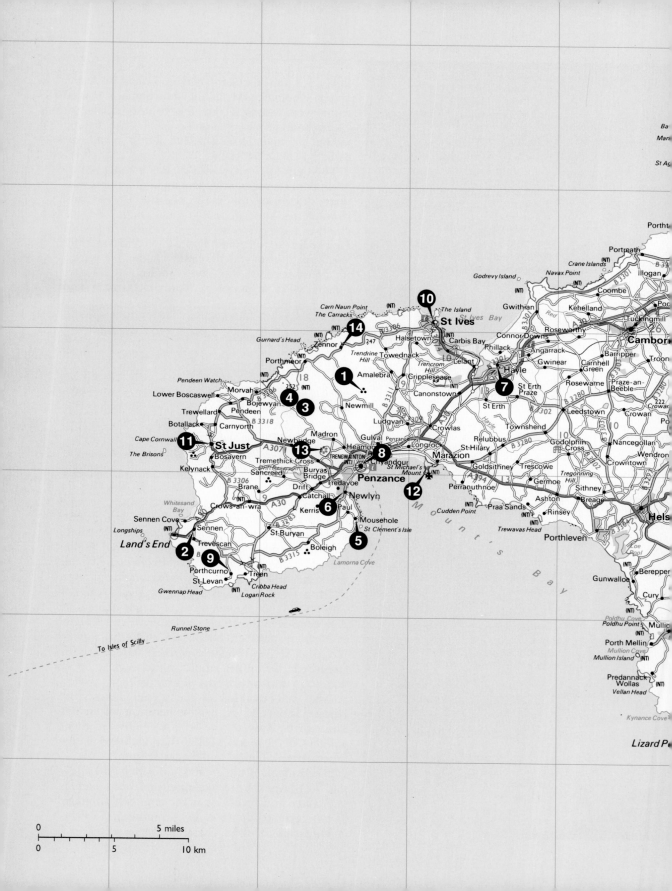

❶ CHYSAUSTER

Although abandoned for about 1800 years, it is still possible to make out the nine houses of Chysauster Iron-Age village. It was inhabited from about 100 BC well into the 2nd century. The site gives the visitor a fascinating insight into how the Iron-Age villagers lived.

❷ LAND'S END THEME PARK

Land's End Theme Park at Sennen has shows on the marine history, wildlife and geology of Land's End. There is an hotel and also a craft centre where you can watch glassblowers, woodcarvers and silversmiths at work. (Open all year daily. Phone 0736 871501)

❸ LANYON QUOIT

Cornwall's famous Neolithic chamber-tomb is the most visited megalith in the West Country. The stones were once known as the Giant's Quoit or the Giant's Table due to the fact that the stones form a huge three-legged table.

❹ MEN-AN-TOL STONES

Also known as the Devil's Eye, these large hoop-like stones with hollow centres were once believed to have healing powers. The stones may once have been the entrance to a Neolithic burial chamber.

❺ MOUSEHOLE

Pronounced 'Mouzell', Mousehole's terraces of picturesque cottages look down on a tiny, steep-walled harbour. In the churchyard at Paul, a mile away, there is a memorial to Dolly Pentreath (died 1777), said to have been the last person to speak only Cornish. The cave known as the 'Mousehole' is found just south of the town, near Point Spaniard.

❻ NEWLYN

A favourite haunt of artists for over a century, Newlyn is also Cornwall's leading fishing port. The 15th-century pier is flanked with Victorian harbour walls and rows of fishing cottages. The Newlyn Art Gallery shows examples of work by local artists past and present. (Open all year, Mon–Sat. Phone 0736 63715)

❼ PARADISE PARK, HAYLE

A refuge for rare and endangered birds, including jewel-coloured parrots and the Cornish chough, a red-billed bird that once inhabited the coast but is now almost extinct. (Open all year daily. Phone 0736 753365)

❽ PENZANCE

Penzance became a fashionable resort in Regency times. Many shops and other buildings have retained their original 18th- or 19th-century fronts, such as the Georgian Egyptian House, now the headquarters of the National Trust. The Maritime Museum features many interesting items salvaged from 18th-century shipwrecks. (Open Easter, May–Oct. Phone 0736 68890) Penlee House Museum has exhibits relating to the natural history of the area as well as illustrating the importance of the region's mining and fishing industries. (Open all year, Mon–Fri and Sat afternoon. Phone 0736 63625)

❾ PORTHCURNO

On top of the granite cliffs overlooking this small, sheltered cove stands the Grecian-style amphitheatre of the Minack Open Air Theatre, used for performances during the summer. If you walk east from Porthcurno, along the coastal path, you'll come to the Iron-Age cliff fort of Treryn Dinas. There is a 66-ton Logan rock here which can be moved with one hand if you find the correct pivotal point.

❿ ST IVES

St Ives was once Cornwall's busiest pilchard fishing port. Tin and copper from nearby mines were also exported from here. The narrow streets behind the wharf were divided into 'Downalong', where the fishing families lived, and 'Upalong', the homes of the miners. Some of the prettiest cottages are found in a street called The Digey, not far from the old artists' and fishermen's inn, The Sloop. These days St Ives is a popular holiday resort with many shops and cafés as well as excellent beaches.

Barbara Hepworth was one of the leaders of the second wave of artists to settle in St Ives. The house in Back Street where she lived from 1949 until her death in 1975 is now the Barbara Hepworth Museum and Sculpture Garden, where you can see her work. (Open all year daily. Phone 0736 796226) The St Ives Museum has many exhibits relating to the town's nautical history, including the clockwork mechanism from Pendeen lighthouse. (Open mid May–Sept daily. Phone 0736 795575) ☎ 0736 796297

⓫ ST JUST-IN-PENWITH

St Just, not to be confused with St Just-in-Roseland, enjoyed its hey-day in Victorian times when it was a busy centre for tin and copper mining. Geevor, the last working mine, is now a museum. (Open Easter–Oct. Phone 0736 788662)

⓬ ST MICHAEL'S MOUNT

Accessible by foot over the causeway at low tide, or by ferry from Marazion, St Michael's Mount is a stunning sight. The original chapel was founded in the 11th century by Edward the Confessor, while the castle was added in the 14th century. Part of the Mount is still the home of Lord St Levan. There is a restaurant and café on the island. (Open Apr–Oct, Mon–Fri. Phone 0736 710507)

⓭ TRENGWAINTON GARDENS

Trengwainton Gardens were established in the 1800s by the son of a wealthy Jamaican sugar plantation owner. A 50-foot (15 m) magnolia tree flowers each spring alongside dense banks of rhododendrons. Camellias, eucalyptus trees and tropical American plants all flourish here. (Open Mar–Oct, Wed–Sat and Bank Hol Mons. ♿. Phone 0736 60400)

⓮ ZENNOR

Legend has it that the son of the local squire was bewitched by the Mermaid of Zennor and lured to her watery home off this spectacular part of the coast. The tale is depicted on the bench end of a seat in the local church. For a glimpse of Cornish cottage life, visit the Wayside Folk Museum. Refreshments available. (Open Easter–Oct. Phone 0736 796945)

Preceding page: **Cadgwith** (AB)

Marconi Memorial, Poldhu (AB)

Looking north from Lion Rock (JH)

Loe Pool, Pentire (AB)

Mullion Cove (JH)

The village of Landewednack on the Lizard Peninsula is the southernmost parish of Britain, and marks an invisible boundary where the crags of Land's End give way to a gentler yet still impressive terrain.

The character of the Lizard is largely determined by its geology. The pillars, stacks and pinnacles of Kynance Cove are carved by the sea from serpentine rock of every imaginable colour, and on the downs below lie small quarries where the rock is excavated and used in the cottage industry of carving ornaments and souvenirs. In an area almost devoid of industry of any kind, the enterprise is important to the local economy. Even the smallest village has a little store which sells necklaces, beads and baubles fashioned from gemstones as well as gifts made from serpentine, such as lighthouses, eggs and ashtrays. The mineral greenstone, which is as hard as basalt, is another distinctive rock found in the area; Mullion owes its picture-book charm to this mineral. It was used to build the harbour walls.

The Lizard Peninsula is the historic, if unlikely, birthplace of several important milestones in the history of science. On the cliffs of Poldhu Cove, overlooking Mount's Bay, there stands a simple, granite column monument to Guglielmo Marconi. The inventor erected a wireless station here in 1900 (now demolished) and on 12 December 1901 sent out the first radio signals to be received

Porthleven harbour (JH)

Lizard Point (JH)

Shetland ponies, Chynalls Cliffs (AB)

across the Atlantic in Newfoundland. (The type of rock formation found in the Peninsula is very stable and therefore ideal as a base from which to send or receive radio signals.) Wireless telegraphy was also developed at the station, and subsequently played a vital role in World War I. The Marconi-Franklin beam system was transmitted from Poldhu in 1924 and further revolutionized long-range radio communication. The saucers of the nearby Goonhilly Down satellite tracking and communication centre represent the progress that has been made since Marconi's early experiments.

The Lizard has some of the rarest of Britain's native wild plants, including Cornish heath, pygmy rush, orchids and unusual varieties of buttercup 17

Helston Furry Dance (AB)

Glendurgan (AB)

Wheale Coates Mine, St Agnes (AB)

and clover. Wild asparagus grows near Kynance Cove. The area is rewarding for birdlovers too, with kestrels, buzzards and ravens supplementing the more common flocks of gulls. Puffins are also sometimes seen here. Sandpipers and godwits inhabit the estuary flats.

The coastal waters are noted for their whelks, crabs and lobsters. Whales and dolphins also visit the coast from time to time, as do basking sharks. Grey seals breed on inaccessible stony beaches and in sea caves along the south coast.

Turning inland, the landscape has many reminders of the area's industrial past, and especially of Cornwall's former status as one of the most prosperous tin and copper mining areas in the world. The area around Camborne and Redruth is the most densely populated in Cornwall. Neither the towns themselves nor their environs could be described as picturesque, but they have a lot to offer if you are interested in industrial archaelogy, mining or engineering. Around the end of the last century, there were literally hundreds of mines in

Goonhilly Satellite Station (JH)

Trebah Gardens (AB)

operation hereabouts, as well as many factories producing ancillary goods to service the mines. The economic situation of the area changed radically when the price of Cornish copper and tin plummeted as a result of cheaper foreign imports. Many miners and their families were forced to seek a new life elsewhere and emigrated to America, Australia and South Africa. The fall in tin prices on the world market in recent years sounded the death-knell for the last vestiges of the industry in Cornwall. The crumbling engine-houses around Pendeen, Camborne and Redruth tell their story to each new generation of visitors, as do the many old mines that have been turned into museums.

Winston Graham drew on historical fact for his *Poldark* novels and these give some idea of the extent of the social and economic changes experienced by the Cornish people during this difficult period in their history. The village of St Ann in the novel is based on the former tin-mining centre of St Agnes.

❶ CADGWITH

Cadgwith is a small, picturesque fishing village of traditional cottages. The local fishermen now specialize in catching lobsters and crabs. In the last century, however, the village was an important centre for pilchard fishing. It is reputed that a catch of 1,300,000 fish was recorded in a single day. About a mile south of Cadgwith is the spectacular Devil's Frying Pan, formed when a sea cave collapsed many centuries ago.

❷ CAMBORNE

Camborne and the surrounding area were once the scene of intensive mining activity and are now a treasure-trove of industrial archaeology. In the 1850s, two-thirds of the world's copper was produced here by 350 mines and 50,000 miners. Inventor Richard Trevithick, 'father of the railway', was born here in 1771 and is honoured each April in a colourful Trevithick-day celebration. At nearby Pool are the East Pool Cornish Beam Engines, a museum set up to preserve these once famous engines. (Open Apr–Oct. Phone 0208 4281) The School of Mines Museum, just outside Camborne, has an extensive collection of minerals from around the world. (Open Mon–Wed, Fri afternoon and Sat morning)

❸ COVERACK

This pretty village with thatched cottages and a tiny pier was once a smuggling centre. Coverack's lifeboat station, which was closed in the 1960s, performed sterling service over the years, rescuing sailors from ships wrecked on the notorious Manacle Rocks farther along the coast.

❹ CULDROSE AIR STATION

South of Helston is the Royal Naval Air Station where Sea-King helicopter pilots are trained. There is a public viewing area adjacent to the car park. Every last Wednesday in July there is an impressive air day.

❺ FLAMBARDS VILLAGE AND CORNWALL AERO PARK

Flambards Village is an authentic re-creation of Victorian shops, streets and homes. The exhibition is set amid landscaped gardens and lakes, complete with children's rides. The aero display features helicopters, a Concorde flight-deck and wartime exhibits. (Open Easter–Oct daily. ♿. Phone 0326 564093)

❻ GOONHILLY SATELLITE STATION

On Goonhilly Downs, ancient landforms meet high-tech. The 11 massive dish-aerials of British Telecom's Goonhilly complex, used to pick up television signals and telephone messages from satellites, are situated in an area containing several burial mounds dating from the Bronze Age. There is a visitor centre. (Open Easter–Sept daily. Phone 0872 78551)

❼ GWEEK

Situated just at the head of the peaceful Helford river, Gweek became the leading port in the area in the 14th century after Helston, the former major port, became landlocked. Tin was mined in the area from the 13th century onwards, but Gweek's trade declined as nearby Truro and Falmouth grew in importance. The village is also well known for its Seal Sanctuary where injured seals washed up on the coast are cared for and kept in five large open-air pools. (Open all year daily. Phone 0326 22361)

❽ HELSTON

Perhaps the best time to visit Helston is 8 May, when the local people dance the famous Furry Dance, a sort of formal jig to welcome spring. Helston was a thriving river port until the 13th century when shingle blocked the channel. In Elizabethan times it became one of Cornwall's four stannary towns, where all the smelted tin mined in the area was brought for testing or assaying. The town has many Regency buildings; you'll find good examples in Cross Street. The Folk Museum, formerly the Old Butter Market (Church Street), has exhibits of Helston's main industries in the 19th and early 20th centuries,

namely mining, quarrying and fishing. (Open Mon–Sat and Wed afternoon. Phone 0326 564027) Loe Pool, 2 miles (3 km) south of Helston, is an unusual example of the 'drowned valleys' found in Devon and Cornwall. Formed by accumulating shingle, this is Cornwall's largest lake.

❾ KENNACK SANDS

With its wide sands and shallow pools, Kennack is an ideal beach for families with young children.

❿ KYNANCE COVE

The dramatic serpentine formations of Kynance Cove inspired many Victorian artists. You can see why, for the amber sands, crystal waters, multicoloured rocks and sea caves are magnificent.

⓫ MULLION

This village is renowned for its 15th-century church. Take a look at the benchends carved with bawdy scenes in the 16th century. The harbour walls are made from local greenstone that sparks when struck with steel.

⓬ POLDARK MINE

There's a working beam engine and a good collection of mining artefacts at this 18th-century tin mine. (Open Apr–Oct daily. ♿. Phone 0326 573173)

⓭ PORTHTOWAN

A centre for surfers, this broad, flat beach with its high, powerful waves is strictly for the experts and can be a dangerous place for novices. Watch for warning flags.

⓮ REDRUTH

With Camborne, Redruth formed the epicentre of Cornish mining and is still one of the busiest industrial towns in Cornwall. Redruth has a cornucopia of architectural styles, ranging from Georgian to Thirties' Art Deco.

⓯ TREBAH GARDENS

The main feature of the gardens is its extensive collection of rare and sub-tropical plants. There is also a water garden here stocked with Koi carp. (Open all year daily. ♿. Phone 0326 250448)

Newquay

Fistral Beach (AB)

Padstow harbour (WCTB)

Newquay harbour (AB)

Preceding page: **Perranporth beach** (AB)   **Mawgan Porth** (JH)

Camel estuary, Padstow (JH)

Evening mist, Doyden (AB)

This somewhat isolated part of Cornwall has a fierce, wild and inhospitable coastline. Inland, narrow country lanes cut across an austere, treeless landscape that is quintessentially Cornish. The railway that used to bring visitors to Padstow was closed in 1966 and transport facilities are now poor so it helps to have your own. If you do have a car, the north Devon link road has made this area and much of Cornwall more accessible.

The area is attractive to those who like traditional holiday pastimes, such as swimming and sunbathing; the sandy beaches of Newquay, northern Cornwall's largest resort, are ideal for these. Alternatively, you can pit yourself against the waves on Fistral Beach, which offers what is said to be the best surfing in the country. The surfing beaches in this area are now famous worldwide and the venue for the world surfing championships.

Pilchard fishing used to be Newquay's biggest industry (now it's tourism) and the most picturesque part of the town is its 17th-century harbour. Some of the pilot gigs that used to guide the cargo schooners safely into port are displayed here. Out on the western headland is the Huer's Hut. Here, a man called a huer would look out for shoals of pilchards swimming into the bay. When the water turned a tell-tale red, a sure sign of the approaching pilchards, he would let out a cry to raise the fishermen of Newquay for the catch.

Wadebridge has a long and colourful history. The Romans are believed to have crossed the River Camel here because there was a ford, or vadum. By the Middle Ages so many travellers and pilgrims were passing through the town that chapels were built and alms collected from them.

River Camel, Wadebridge (WCTB)

Holywell Bay, near Newquay (AB)

Trerice House (AB)

It was not until the 15th century that a town bridge was built in Wadebridge. Many tales are told about the building of this bridge, which Carew described as 'the longest, strongest and fairest bridge that the Shire can muster'. The bridge was known as the Bridge on Wool, because tradition has it that the foundations were laid on packs of wool to give the bridge stability; this explanation isn't as far-fetched as it sounds, for wool solidifies when it is wet and compressed. Another possibility is that the money to construct the bridge came from wealthy local sheep farmers; Wadebridge was an important wool trading centre at this time.

Some good walks are to be had from Wadebridge. The route of the old railway line linking the town to Padstow is now a footpath and offers a pleasant, scenic walk. Alternatively, you could follow the course of the river, along the Camel trail. This 10-mile walk and cycleway runs between Wadebridge and Bodmin. For three days each June the town plays host to the Royal Cornwall Show, the major agricultural and general event of the year.

Lobster fisherman, Port Isaac (AB)

Watergate Bay, near Newquay (JH)

Cornwall was one of the first parts of England to be converted to Christianity, hence the old saying 'there are more saints in Cornwall than were ever enthroned in heaven'. Cornwall had already been Christian for over a century when St Augustine arrived in Kent, in AD 597, to begin the task of converting the heathen Anglo-Saxons. Padstow was a centre of early Christianity. St Petroc arrived here from Ireland in AD 518 to found a monastery. The overland route between Padstow and Fowey, on the north coast (the embarkation point for the Continent), was allegedly known as the Saints' Way or 'Forth an Syns', such was the volume of saintly traffic. Dotted along the Saints' Way were ancient shrines, burial chambers and medieval churches as well as some of Cornwall's famous holy wells, many of which can still be seen today.

The May Day celebrations in Padstow are an ancient tradition and have much to do with the town's fishing past. The festivities last for one or two days, and include much dancing in the streets. There's even a traditional song which goes with the event.

27

❶ BEDRUTHAN STEPS

Legend has it that these huge lumps of granite were once the stepping stones of Bedruthan, the giant who appears in the fairytale *Jack and the Beanstalk*.

❷ CORNISH SHIRE HORSE CENTRE

Over 30 shire horses take part in regular parades every day at the centre. There is also an indoor arena, blacksmith's shop, museum and cart rides. Restaurant. (Open Easter–Oct. ⚹. Phone 0841 540276)

❸ CRANTOCK

A traditional village of colour-washed cottages, Crantock is separated from Newquay by a long, narrow estuary called the Gannel. A plaque records that the village stocks, which stand outside the church, were last used on a 'smuggler's son and a vagabond' in 1817. Nearby Crantock Beach is a very popular stretch of sand.

❹ DAIRYLAND

Dairyland is a popular farm park with wildfowl, pheasants and a museum of country life. It also has an adventure playground and farm nature trail. (Open Easter–Oct daily. ⚹. Phone 0872 510246)

❺ HOLYWELL BEACH

A quiet beach with good bathing except at low tide. It is named after a freshwater spring, found at the north end of the beach.

❻ LAPPA VALLEY STEAM RAILWAY

Here you can take a 2-mile return trip by miniature steam loco-motives on a 15-inch gauge line, originally part of the track used by the Great Western Railway. Alight at East Wheal Rose Halt for the boating lake, maze and children's leisure park. (Open mid Apr–Sept daily. ⚹. Phone 0872 510643)

❼ NEWQUAY

Over the years, since the completion of the railway in 1875, Newquay, with its wide, sweeping beaches has become one of the most popular resorts in Cornwall. The 17th-century harbour has remained unspoilt due to its relatively small size. Although large enough to take the schooners of the 19th century, the shallow harbour was not big enough to take larger cargo boats. Just to the west of the town lies Trenance Park. Its 8 acres of land-scaped parklands are home to the recently completed indoor Water-world and Newquay Zoo, the only full-size zoo in Cornwall. As well as a variety of swimming pools and water slides, there is a Tarzan trail, maze and garden and the usual range of wild animals, such as bears, big cats, monkeys, seals and penguins. (Open all year daily) Trenance Cottage Museum situated in the centre of the park has an impressive collection of antiques and objets d'arts gathered from all over the world. (Open Easter–mid Oct) ☎ 0637 871345

❽ PADSTOW

Padstow was an early centre of Christianity, and St Petroc (the name Padstow is derived from Petrocstowe) is said to have founded a monastery here in the 6th century. It is thought that the monastery was situated in an area now occupied by Prideaux Place, an attractive Elizabethan house; the interior includes the Great Chamber, which has a fine embossed plaster ceiling dated 1585. There is also 20-acre deer park. (Open Easter; Spring Bank Hol–Sept, afternoons only. Phone 0841 532411) The town celebrates Mayday with the Hobby Horse Dance Festival. As part of the festivities, a masked man on a hobby horse dances through the streets. The Tropical Bird Garden has a wonderful collection of birds and butterflies. (Open all year daily. Phone 0841 532262)

❾ PERRANPORTH

Perranporth is a popular holiday resort with a 3-mile long, sandy beach as one of its main attractions. In the 6th century the patron saint of tinners, St Piran, founded a chapel on Penhale Sands a mile north of the town; but by the 11th century the shifting sand-dunes had completely covered the building. It remained hidden until it was excavated in 1835.

❿ POLZEATH

Former Poet Laureate Sir John Betjeman spent many childhood holidays here and is buried in the Church of St Enodoc. The sandy beaches of Polzeath offer safe bathing, as well as good surfing, and are ideal for families with young children.

⓫ PORT ISAAC

Lofty headlands flank the pic-turesque village of Port Isaac, which has been a fishing com-munity since the Middle Ages. The narrow alleyways and huddled rows of slate cottages, overlooking the harbour, are largely unspoilt.

⓬ ST MAWGAN

Set amid the wooded landscape of the Vale of Lanherne, St Mawgan is renowned for its pretty cottages, its twin bridges and the 16th-century Falcon Inn. In the village there is a boat-shaped memorial to ten shipwrecked seamen whose bodies were washed ashore at Mawgan Porth, a sheltered cove lying at the foot of the vale; the beach here is ideal for bathing.

⓭ TRERICE HOUSE

Several miles south of Newquay stands the National Trust-owned Elizabethan manor, Trerice. Built of local limestone in 1571 by the Arundell family, it features Dutch-style gables, Elizabethan plaster-work and many fine paintings. There is also a huge 15th-century barn containing a collection of lawn-mowers! (Open Apr–Oct daily. Phone 0637 875404)

⓮ WADEBRIDGE

The town takes its name from its medieval bridge (c 1485), said to be one of the finest in Britain. The structure is 320 feet (98 m) long and has 17 arches. It was widened in 1849.

⓯ WORLD IN MINIATURE

A collection of miniature copies of the world's most famous statues and buildings, set in 12 acres of landscaped gardens. One of the exhibits is of a Western street scene and called 'Tombstone'. (Open mid Mar–mid Oct daily. Phone 0872 572828)

South Cornwall

Lanhydrock House (AB)

Mevagissey harbour (JH)

Preceding page: **Pendennis Castle, Falmouth** (JH)

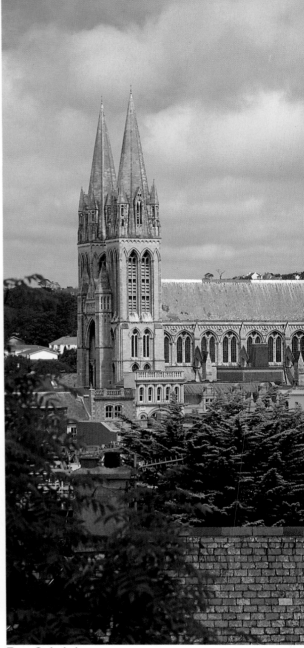

Truro Cathedral (JH)

All along the coast, from Falmouth to Fowey, shady creeks, narrow winding inlets and wooded waterways make this area of Cornwall one of the most attractive in the county. The waters round here are the home of Morgawr (Cornish for the 'sea giant'), the Cornish version of the Loch Ness Monster, which is said to have a humped back and horns.

The legend of Tristan and Iseult is associated with this part of Cornwall. The ill-fated lovers were doomed to follow the dictates of a hopeless passion as a result of drinking a potion intended for Iseult and her future husband, King Mark of Cornwall. The legend may be based on a true story. King Mark is said to have lived at Castle Dore at Lantyan in the 6th century; the remains of an ancient castle can be seen here. And near Fowey there is a stone inscribed with the earliest known form of the name Tristan.

The thickly wooded Luxulyan valley north of St Blaizey is a favourite beauty spot with visitors and locals. A huge viaduct built by local mine owner,

Churchyard, St Just-in-Roseland (JH)

Pendennis Castle (JH)

Round House, Veryan (AB)

Joseph Treffry, in 1842 to carry water and ore across the valley to the port of Par is still standing. You can walk to the top of the viaduct; it's quite a climb, but well worth it for the view of the valley.

Fowey (pronounced 'Foy'), an historic town overlooking the beautiful Fowey estuary, had a long association with one of Cornwall's most famous literary figures, Sir Arthur Quiller-Couch. The son of a Cornish doctor, Sir Arthur, or 'Q' as he was known to his readers, first came to prominence as editor of the *Oxford Book of*

33

Bodinnick ferryhouse, Fowey (AB)   **St Mawes' Castle** (AB)   **Wheal Martyn Museum** (WCTB)

Carrick Roads, Falmouth (AB)

English Verse. Fowey appears in his writings thinly disguised as 'Troy Town'. Such was the popularity of his books in Edwardian times that visitors flocked to the town.

Another writer whose lifelong association with Cornwall also began in Fowey is Daphne du Maurier. She was instantly captivated by the place when she first arrived here as a young woman in the late Twenties. Her first home in the area was Ferryside, which overlooks the water at Bodinnick; the house is still there. Later, she moved to Menabilly, near Polkerris, where she found the inspiration for her most famous novel, *Rebecca*.

Throughout the Middle Ages and well into the 18th century Cornish roads were too rutted and narrow to permit much transport, and most goods and cargo were moved from place to place by river or sea. Cornwall's unofficial capital, Truro, thrived on this trade. The city, England's smallest, stands on an inlet of the huge Fal estuary, where the rivers Allen and Kenwyn meet. It rapidly became a prosperous stannary town from where ore mined in the local villages was transported. Eventually, though, the river traffic ground to a halt; deposits of silt that had gradually been building up formed sandbanks and bars, making the estuary impassable. The ore then had to be transported by road to working ports. The mining boom of the 18th century brought fresh economic impetus, and many wealthy families moved into the town. You can see examples of the elegant houses built in the city at this time in Lemon Street and Walsingham Place. The centre of modern Truro is pedestrianized and offers good and easy shopping.

St Austell is the capital of the china-clay industry and has been a prominent industrial centre for over a century. The china-clay (or kaolin) deposits at St Austell were first discovered in 1755, by William Cookworthy. Initially used in the manufacture of porcelain, china clay is now also used for adding special finishes to paper and for making various kinds of paints and medicines. The first sight that used to greet visitors as they approached the town was the stretch of ghostly, almost lunar, waste heaps of china-clay sand, dubbed the 'Cornish Alps'. English China Clays, the main kaolin producers, eventually decided to do something about this eyesore and set about planting the heaps with grass and shrubs. The company's grassed waste tips are now home to a specially imported breed of mountain goat which thrives on the terrain.

❶ FALMOUTH

Falmouth, sited on the estuaries of seven rivers, became one of Britain's busiest ports in the 17th century when it was made a Mail Packet Station. From this time on the town's importance as a centre of communication with the Empire grew until the packet service was moved to Southampton in the late 19th century, taking much of Falmouth's prosperity with it. However, with the arrival of the railway in 1863 Falmouth soon became a popular holiday resort. The famous round Pendennis Castle, built by Henry VIII, was the last Royalist stronghold in the Civil War, before falling to Cromwell's forces after a 5-month siege. (Open Apr–Sept daily; Oct–Mar, Tues–Sun) The Falmouth Maritime Museum (Bell's Court) has exhibits relating to the town's seafaring past, including the Falmouth Packet Service. Part of the museum is housed on the steam tug *St Denys* (Custom House Quay); the exhibits concentrate on engineering (Museum open all year daily, except Sun in winter; tug open Easter–Sept, Sun–Fri) The Falmouth Art Gallery has a collection of paintings by artists such as Waterhouse, Munnings and the local painter Henry Scott Tuke. (Open all year, Mon–Fri. Phone 0326 313863) ☎ 0326 312300

❷ FOWEY

This quiet port overlooking the Fowey estuary has many houses dating from the 16th century, mainly in the area around the market hall and 14th-century church. A passenger ferry runs to Polruan. ☎ 0726 833616

❸ LANHYDROCK HOUSE

Lanhydrock, in high Victorian style, was largely rebuilt in the 1890s after a fire destroyed much of the 17th-century original. Thirty-six rooms are open to the public, most notable of which is the 116-foot (36 m) gallery with its intricate plaster-work ceiling. The attractive formal garden was laid out in 1837. Restaurant. (Open Apr–Oct daily, except house closed Mon; Nov–Mar, garden only open) ☎ Bodmin 0208 76616

❹ LOSTWITHIEL

The old stannary town of Lostwithiel was the capital of Cornwall in the 13th century. As well as many antique and craft shops the town has an interesting history museum (Open Easter–Oct) Just north of Lostwithiel is Restormel Castle. Originally the site of a Norman castle, it was rebuilt in the Middle Ages. Abandoned in the 16th century, the castle is now a ruin. (Open Apr–Sept daily, Oct–Mar, Tues–Sun. Phone 0208 872687)

❺ LUXULYAN

This remote hill-top village overlooking Luxulyan valley, has some striking cottages and a 15th-century church. Also in the village is St Cyor's holy well – now dried up.

❻ MEVAGISSEY

Mevagissey's colour-washed cottages line the valley overlooking the harbour. The town has a folk museum with exhibitions on local occupations and a reconstruction of a 19th-century Cornish kitchen. (Open Easter–Sept, Mon–Fri and weekend afternoons. Phone 0726 843568) There is also an extensive model railway. (Open Easter, summer months daily; winter, Sun only. ♿ Phone 0726 842457)

❼ ST AUSTELL

St Austell, although the centre of the china-clay industry, has a pleasant market town feel. The parish church of Holy Trinity has a 15th-century tower, one of the finest in Cornwall.

❽ ST JUST-IN-ROSELAND

Hidden away in a tiny creek off the Carrick Roads, this hamlet has an attractive churchyard. A walk to the church takes you through a wooded combe thick with hydrangeas as well as more exotic plants.

❾ ST MAWES

The smart, whitewashed cottages and villas of St Mawes rise up steeply from its busy harbour. St Mawes has one of the largest round castles in England, the twin of Pendennis Castle. Both castles were built by Henry VIII. (Open all year daily. Phone 0326 316594)

❿ TRELISSICK GARDENS

Trelissick Gardens are set in classic Cornish countryside. Impressive grounds and woodlands surround the garden, which contains many different varieties of plants. Also in the grounds are a National Trust shop and restaurant. (Open Mar–Oct, Mon–Sat and Sun afternoons. Phone 0872 862090 ♿)

⓫ TREWITHEN HOUSE AND GARDENS

Described as Cornwall's most beautiful garden, Trewithen has many rare plants. The 17th-century house was rebuilt (1715–1755) by the architect Thomas Edwards. Every room has highly individual decor, ranging from English oak panelling to intricate Chinese fretwork. (Gardens open Mar–Sept, Mon–Sat. House open Apr–Jul, Mon and Tues only. Phone 0726 882764)

⓬ TRURO

The Assembly Rooms and the houses in Lemon Street date from the 18th century and are reminders of the town's prosperity at this time. The crescent of Walsingham Place, built early in the 19th century, is equally elegant. Truro's famous cathedral (1880–1910) stands on the site of the 16th-century church of St Mary. It has a richly carved interior with narrow columns ascending to a vaulted ceiling. The County Museum (River Street) has a famous collection of Cornish minerals, Japanese ivories and lacquer work and English pottery and porcelain. (Open all year, Mon–Sat. Phone 0872 72205)

⓭ VERYAN

Legend has it that the five round houses here were designed by a local vicar for his daughters. The houses were constructed in the round so that the devil would have no corners to hide in!

⓮ WHEAL MARTYN MUSEUM

This restored Victorian clay works has working water wheels and a steam locomotive. There is also an exhibition of china-clay industry artefacts, equipment, clothes and locomotives. (Open Apr–Oct daily; Bank Hols. Phone 0726 850362)

37

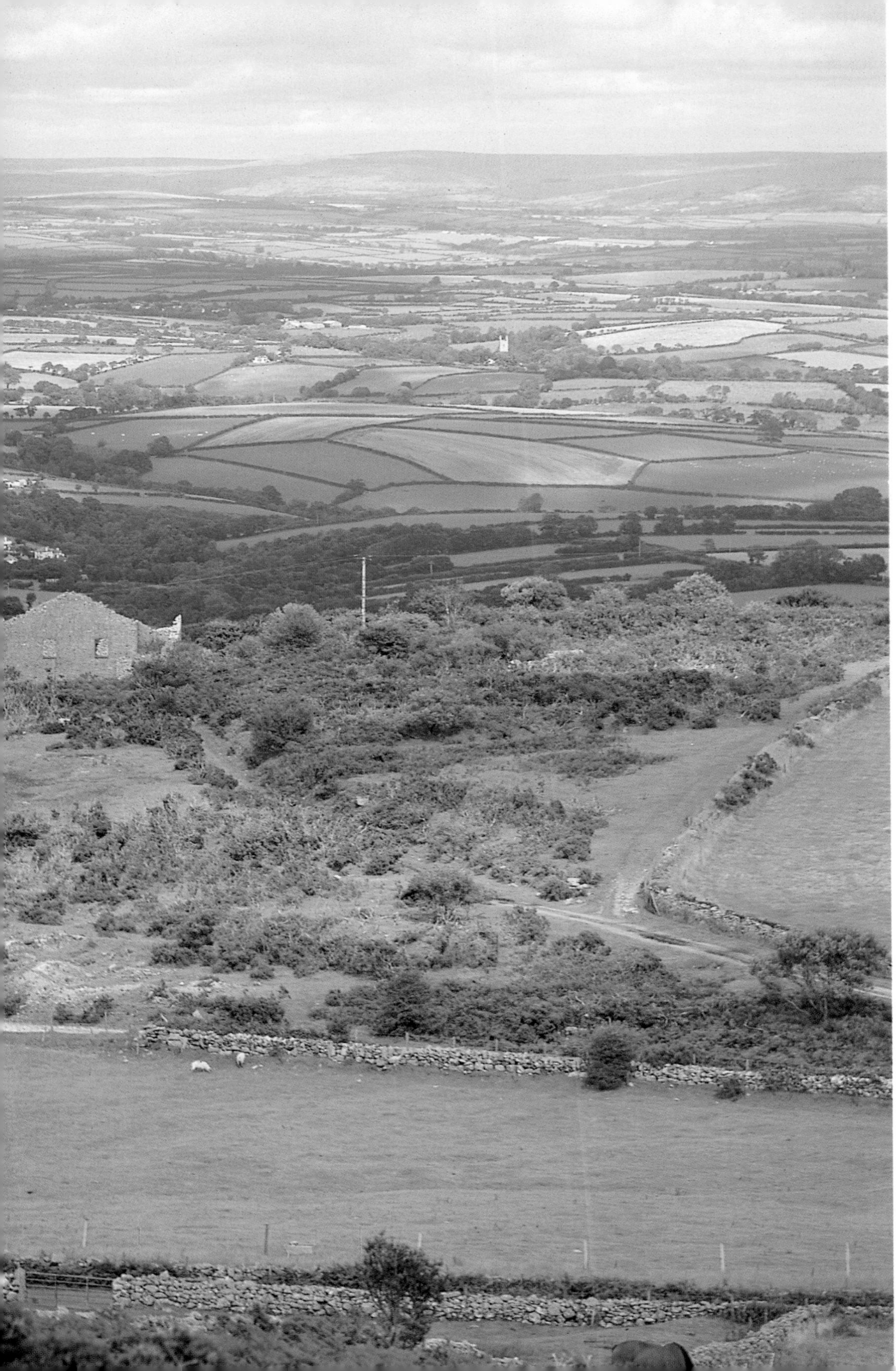

Bodmin to Bude

Preceding page: **Looking east from Minions** (JH)

The windswept, desolate moorlands of Bodmin are among the remotest inland areas of Cornwall. The main A30 road cuts through its centre, but only if you leave this route and venture along the narrow tracks leading off it will you discover signs of human habitation. The moor is privately owned by, among others, the Duke of Cornwall and Lord Falmouth. Sheep and horses have rights to wander; the rest of us are required to keep to the few public footpaths. If you like walking but prefer a less bleak landscape than this one, the woods around Bodmin town itself offer an attractive alternative.

Bodmin is the county town of Cornwall and as such has much of interest for the visitor, including the jail, steam railway, farm park and the Light Infantry Museum. The parish church, St Petroc's (1472), is the largest in Cornwall. Every first Saturday in July the townspeople of Bodmin hang their mayor. This symbolic gesture dates back to 1549 and the Prayer Book Rebellion. The then mayor of Bodmin, Nicholas Boyer, was one of the

Tintagel Castle (AB)

Old Post Office, Tintagel (AB)

Interior of Blisland Church (AB)

Tintagel (AB)

leaders of the rebellion. The uprising spread as far as Exeter before the authorities in London took action, sending the Provost-Marshal, Sir Anthony Kingston, to sort out the problem. Over dinner Sir Anthony ordered the mayor to erect the town gallows because there was someone he wanted to hang. No sooner was this done than Boyer found himself on the end of the rope! The annual re-enactment of the hanging does not involve the active participation of the real mayor; a local stand-in is used instead.

The area around Bodmin Moor is famous for its slate quarrying. The industry is over six centuries old and still alive, although the number of miners employed has fallen considerably in recent years. Delabole, the largest slate quarry in Britain, used to give employment to 500 men, but now there are jobs for only 50.

Many great stories and legends have originated in this part of Cornwall, including one of the most famous of them all, the story of King Arthur. The medieval writer Geoffrey of Monmouth, who

Churchyard, Morwenstow (AB)

Cheesewring, Bodmin (JH)

Pencarrow House (AB)

Boscastle harbour (AB)

42

recorded the legends and stories of his time, was the first authority to state that Arthur was born and died in this area. Each year thousands of visitors flock to the small town of Tintagel, allegedly Arthur's birthplace, which is now the centre of a massive 'King Arthur' industry. Archaeologists and historians have found evidence of a Celtic royal household near Tintagel, but nothing in Tintagel itself. Tintagel Castle certainly looks as though it ought to have been Arthur's family home, but this cannot be the case because it was built much later, by the Normans.

Another site associated with Arthur is Castle-an-Dinas, near St Columb. The castle became the seat of Cornish kings after Arthur's death, and is the largest Celtic hill fort in Cornwall. It is now owned by the Cornwall Heritage Trust.

Dozmary Pool (JH)

The valley of the River Camel lent its name to Arthur's kingdom, Camelot. Arthur is said to have fought his last battle at Slaughter Bridge, near Camelford. It is said that the waters of the Camel ran red, so great was the bloodshed. Sir Bevidere was promptly despatched to the magical lake of Dozmary Pool, 6 miles (10 km) away to return Arthur's sword, Excalibur, to the water. The fatally wounded king was then borne away to the narrow harbour of nearby Boscastle, where his funeral barge waited to carry him to Avalon.

Bodmin Moor was the home of the greatest villain in Cornish legend, Jan Tregeagle. The steward of the Lord of Lanhydrock in the 16th century, Tregeagle was supposed to have made his

Parson Hawker's hut, Morwenstow (AB)

The Haven, Bude (AB)

Disused mine workings, Bodmin (JH)

Cliffs at Morwenstow (AB)

View across Bodmin (JH)

fortune by marrying a succession of heiresses and then murdering them. He's also said to have killed his own children and, finally, sold his soul to the Devil. The ghost of Tregeagle was condemned to baling out Dozmary Pool with a limpet shell. On wild, stormy nights when the moon is full, it's said that Tregeagle is hunted across the moor by the Devil and a pack of diabolic hounds.

The Cornish custom of smuggling has a long association with Bodmin. Cornish families involved in piracy during the 15th and 16th centuries quite easily turned their hands to dealing in contraband in the 18th century when their original 'business' was stamped out. Smuggling is the theme of Daphne du Maurier's novel, *Jamaica Inn*. The action takes place in Bolventor, a tiny, isolated hamlet and an ideal rendezvous for smugglers. In her memoirs the novelist described how she and her companion set out for Jamaica Inn on horseback, only to get lost on the moors. In the novel, Du Maurier recreates this frightening experience when her heroine, Mary, also loses her way. Coachloads of tourists have now replaced the bands of smugglers who used to inhabit these parts. Fortunately, they have not managed to destroy the area's atmosphere, as a solitary walk across the moor, past the Bronze-Age settlements and up Brown Willy, Cornwall's highest peak (1377 ft/424 m), will prove.

This part of Cornwall was home to one of the county's most colourful eccentrics, Parson Stephen Hawker (1835–74). He was the subject of a best-selling novel by Baring-Gould, *The Vicar of Morwenstow*. The vicar spent 40 years serving a flock which he described as a 'mixed multitude of smugglers, wreckers and dissenters'. He was greatly worried by the spiritual fate of shipwrecked sailors and would often risk life and limb in retrieving their bodies from the rocks and carrying them back to the village for Christian burial. The parson evidently regarded his pets as part of his flock and expected them to obey the Scriptures — one of his cats was excommunicated for catching a mouse on the Sabbath! Hawker's eccentricity extended to his style of dress. He would stride about Morwenstow in long wellington boots, a seaman's jersey and a purple overcoat. Even more original was his liking for dressing up as a mermaid — on which occasions he favoured this particular outfit we are not sure. He wrote a great deal of poetry, including *The Song of The Western Men* which became the Cornish national anthem.

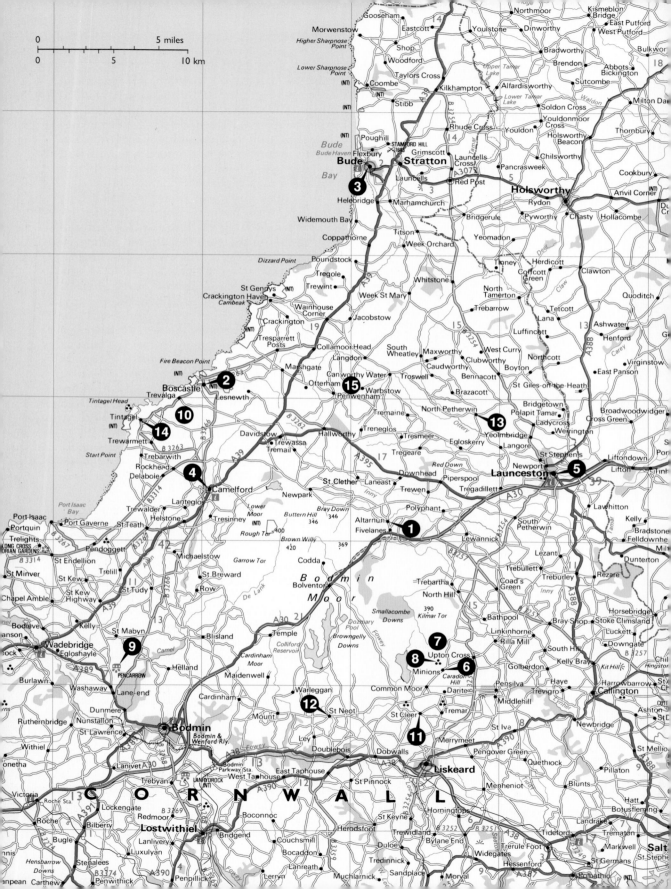

1 ALTARNUN

Altarnun's Church of St Nonna, known as 'The Cathedral of The Moor', has 70 beautifully carved 16th-century bench ends. 1½ miles south of the village, across the A30, lies the Halvana Nature Trail.

2 BOSCASTLE

A narrow, fjord-like entrance leads to Boscastle harbour, where the Valency and Jordan rivers meet the incoming tide, often with dramatic effects; a nearby blow-hole impressively illustrates the force of the water. The village itself has attractive, limewashed cottages lining the steep hillsides. Thomas Hardy often visited Boscastle when he was a young man. Down at the quayside, there is a Museum of Witchcraft which contains many gruesome relics and artefacts. (Opening times not available)

3 BUDE

This once busy port, which served the canal route to Launceston, has been a popular resort since the 19th century. Beyond the replica castle, built in the 1830s and now used by the council, there is an excellent beach suitable for surfing as well as families with young children. The Historical and Folk Museum (The Wharf) has many exhibits describing the history of the town and showing how the famous tub-boat canal worked. (Open Easter–Oct daily. &. ✗. Phone 0288 353576) The canal was built in 1826 and was able to transport boats all the way to the sea. The World of Nature Exhibition has an aquarium and exhibits of the local natural history and geology. (Open all year Mon–Sat, closed Thurs afternoon. ✗. Phone 0228 352423) ✉ 0288 354240

4 CAMELFORD

The peaceful market town of Camelford, reputed to have been the site of Camelot, was once a lively, wool-producing town. The North Cornwall Museum and Gallery reflects the history of Cornish rural life. Displays range from tools used by blacksmiths to pottery. (Open Apr–Sept, Mon–Sat. Phone 0840 212954) Two

miles west of Camelford, just off the B3314, is Delabole Slate Quarry. It is the largest quarry in Britain, 1½ miles (2 km) wide and 500 feet (154 m) deep. You can watch the miners at work from the public viewing platform. The slate is used all over Britain for a wide range of domestic purposes as well as for church altars and flooring.

5 LAUNCESTON

Launceston is dominated by its castle, which stands on a high mound on a ridge overlooking this attractive town. The castle was the principal stronghold of William the Conqueror's half-brother, Robert of Mortain. The huge, round keep, gatehouses and some of the walls are still standing. (Open all year daily. ✗. Phone 0566 772365) Launceston has some very fine buildings dating from the 16th and 18th centuries. There are also many interesting Georgian houses including Lawrence House (Castle Street), the local history museum. (Open Apr–mid Oct, Mon–Fri) You can also see the remains of the old town walls, which date from the time of Henry VIII. ✉ 0566 772321

6 – 8 MINIONS

Standing on the southern fringes of Bodmin Moor, Minions was formerly a mining centre from where blue-grey granite was transported to Looe. It is also the site of The Cheesewring, the highest pub in Cornwall. On the edge of Cheesewring granite quarry about a mile north of the village is the Cheesewring itself, a peculiar natural formation of flattish rocks. Just west of Minions is another strange formation, the Hurlers, three Bronze Age stone circles which, according to legend, were men turned to stone as a punishment for playing the Cornish game of hurling on Sunday.

9 PENCARROW HOUSE

Built for Sir John Molesworth in the early 18th century, Pencarrow House contains one of the West Country's best collections of paintings, furniture and china. In the grounds there are woodland gardens, a palm house and a

children's corner. (Open Easter–mid Oct, Sun–Thurs. &. Phone 020884 369)

10 ROCKY VALLEY

Rocky Valley is the site of the 40-foot (12 m) waterfall of St Nectan's Kieve. Nectan, a Celtic hermit and saint, was reputed to have established his oratory beside the kieve or basin.

11 ST CLEER

This group of moorland cottages is built around a 15th-century church close to St Cleer's Well and Trethevy Quoit, a Neolithic chamber tomb. The Doniert Stone is a block of intricately carved granite dedicated to a 9th-century Cornish king who drowned near here.

12 ST NEOT

Lying in a wooded hollow on the edge of Bodmin Moor, St Neot's church contains some of the finest medieval stained glass in England.

13 TAMAR OTTER PARK

Here you can see otters in open enclosures. There are also waterfowl, a woodland trail, deer, pheasants and owls. (Open Apr–Oct daily. ✗. Phone 0566 85646)

14 TINTAGEL

This is the centre of the legend of King Arthur. Tintagel Castle, on the outskirts of the town, is perched on a hilltop overlooking the sea. It was built in the 12th century, and although it has the dramatic setting which legends demand it has no connection with Arthur. (Open Apr–Sept daily, Oct–Mar, Tues–Sun. Phone 0840 770328)

The Old Post Office was set up as a Post Office in 1844, but only to receive incoming mail. Built of slate, clues to its 14th-century origins are provided by the tiny windows, vast fireplaces and galleried interior. The house is furnished with oak pieces made locally. (Open Apr–Oct daily. &)

15 WARBSTOW BURY

This is one of the best examples of an Iron-Age hill fort in Cornwall. It's a good viewpoint too, situated 750 feet (230 m) above sea level.

East Cornwall

Preceding page: **Polperro harbour** (JH)

Sometimes called 'Forgotten Cornwall', this corner of the county will appeal to those who like to 'get away from it all'. East Cornwall has little of the glitter and few of the theme parks that are such features of the resorts farther west. It offers, instead, a landscape and coastline of outstanding natural beauty.

The area was for many centuries isolated by virtue of its geography and poor communications. The River Tamar provided the only link with the outside world for the people living in the villages and hamlets along its banks. You can still sense something of this isolation and remoteness, especially in the winding country paths around Cotehele. A short distance from Cotehele is the village of Calstock, a former mining and ship-building community of immense importance in Victorian times. The village is in a beautiful spot, on a hill overlooking the Tamar. You can take a trip downriver to Plymouth or ride across the spectacular Calstock viaduct on the local train. Calstock also has some good pubs and restaurants.

Communications with the outside world were improved by the installation of a floating bridge

Rose garden, Cotehele House (AB)

Miniature railway, Dobwalls Theme Park (WCTB)

Kitchen at Cotehele (NT)

Cotehele House (AB)

Looe (JH)

over the Tamar, at Saltash, in 1829. Saltash, which means 'the meeting place of salt and water', was for hundreds of years the major ferry port on the river. The tides in the estuary are very strong and the ferry used to be pulled across by means of a chain laid on the river floor. The car ferry that operates between nearby Torpoint and Plymouth works on the same principle. In 1859 a new railway bridge was built in the town. This was an event of some importance, because the project was undertaken by the famous engineer Isambard Kingdom Brunel. Brunel's grandiose, almost eccen-

tric, design is still there, carrying mainline railway traffic into and out of Cornwall. By its side is the 1962 Tamar suspension bridge, which carries four lanes of road traffic. The bridge is now linked to the Saltash road tunnel, which bypasses the town. The tunnel has the distinction of being Europe's most expensive, yard for yard.

The coastal villages of Seaton, Downderry, Crafthole and Portwrinkle are relatively peaceful places even at the height of the season. The coastal path in this area is similarly uncluttered and offers many hours of pleasure to those who like walking. 51

River Tamar, Cotehele (AB)

Shell House, Polperro (JH)

Pencarrow Head (AB)

The *Shamrock* sailing barge, Cotehele Quay (AB)

A half-day circular ramble round Rame Head, using the pretty village of Cawsand as a base, is just one option. The coastal path from the village leads to Penlee Point. You then follow the metalled track until it turns inland. The road leads straight on to Rame Head. The headland was once the site of an Iron-Age fort protected by a deep ditch, which you can still see surrounding the summit. Over the centuries Rame Head has been home to a 14th-century chapel (St Michael's), a hermitage and a light beacon for shipping. The path leading down from Rame Head in the direction of Whitsand Bay was part of the battery and fort system built in the mid 18th century to protect Plymouth Sound and the old Royal Docks. You

Cawsand (WCTB)

can then head back to the linked villages of Cawsand and Kingsand overlooking Cawsand Bay, which was used as an anchoring point by the Royal Navy before Plymouth Breakwater was built.

The villages once stood on either side of the Devon-Cornwall border. Kingsand became part of Cornwall in 1835 and you can still see Halfway House which marks the boundary between the two villages. The fishermen of Cawsand Bay were smugglers as well as enthusiastic pilchard catchers. It's estimated that in 1804 17,000 barrels of spirits passed through Cawsand and Kingsand. This trade was carried on under the nose of Horatio Nelson, who was a regular visitor; he and Lady Hamilton used to stay at the Ship Inn. Cawsand has another Nelson connection. Lieutenant John Pollard of Cawsand was a young midshipman aboard Nelson's flagship *Victory* at the Battle of Trafalgar (1805). He earned the nickname 'Nelson's Avenger' for firing against the French ship *Redoutable* in retaliation for the fatal wounding of his commander.

❶ ANTONY HOUSE

The Carew family and their descendants have lived in this pale grey Queen Anne mansion since it was built around 1711. The interior, including furnishings, has remained virtually untouched since this time. The best way of approaching Antony is by boat, using the ferry from Plymouth. (Open Apr–Oct, Tues, Wed and Thurs; Jun–Aug, Tues, Wed, Thurs and Sun. Phone 0752 812191)

❷ CARNGLAZE SLATE CAVERNS

Established in the 14th century, this now disused quarry once produced quality roofing slate. The slate was cut out of the hillside, leaving two huge caverns; the lower of the two has formed a spectacular underground lake. (Open Easter–Sept daily. Phone 0579 20251)

❸–❹ CAWSAND AND KINGSAND

These twin villages, almost running into each other, overlook Cawsand Bay, which was once used as an anchoring point by the Royal Navy until the Plymouth breakwater was built. For this reason there are many elegant houses dotted around the villages and several old pubs dating from Regency times. Lord Nelson and Lady Hamilton were once regular guests at the Ship Inn.

❺ COTEHELE HOUSE

Building work of the grey, granite manor house of Cotehele was started in 1485 and continued until 1627. The house is particularly notable for its richly embroidered tapestries and hangings. Take the path that leads from the gardens, with its ponds and terraces, through the woods to Cotehele Quay. Here you'll find a small museum with a working watermill, Cotehele Mill. This was the original manorial mill used to grind the corn. There is also a wheelwright's shop and a forge. (Garden and museum open Apr–Oct, daily; House, Apr–Oct, Sat–Thurs; Nov–Mar garden open daily. ♿ Phone 0579 50434)

❻ DOBWALLS THEME PARK

You'll find a number of attractions here. The most interesting is the Forest Railway, a miniature line based on early American railroads with landscape features such as Red Indian tepees, forests, tunnels and canyons. Dobwalls is also home to a museum dedicated to Archibald Thorburn, one of Britain's most distinguished Victorian bird painters. The imaginative exhibition includes tableaux of Victorian scenes and use sound effects to add to the realism of the museum. The park has playgrounds and picnic areas. Refreshments (Open all year daily. ♿ ♿. Phone 0579 20325)

❼ KIT HILL

This 1094-foot (336 m) high viewpoint gives breathtaking panoramic views of the Tamar Valley and Plymouth Sound.

❽ LANREATH FARM MUSEUM

This popular museum features vintage tractors, a variety of engines and other pieces of old farm machinery and implements. There are also demonstrations of traditional rural crafts. (Open Easter–Oct daily. Phone 0503 20321)

❾ LOOE

Looe is situated on both sides of the long harbour at the mouth of the Looe River. The two towns of East and West Looe have been linked by a bridge since 1411 but were not united until 1883. The centre of West Looe is its attractive quay and church of St Nicholas, built with wood salvaged from shipwrecks. You can see reminders of Looe's past as a smuggling centre in the Old Guildhall Museum. (Open Easter–Oct, Mon–Sat. Phone 0503 62072) Looe is also famous for shark and deep sea fishing. About a mile east of Looe is the Murrayton Monkey Sanctuary, where South American woolly monkeys are kept. (Open Easter hols then May–Sept, Sun–Thurs. Phone 0503 62532)

❿ MOUNT EDGCUMBE

The 240-year-old park has many beautiful scenic walks. The 900 acres in which the 16th-century house is set contain a deer park, a folly and formal gardens. Recent additions include a New Zealand Garden and American plantation. The house was badly damaged during World War II but has now been restored in the late 18th-century style. Restaurant. (Park open all year daily; House Apr–Oct, Wed–Sun. Phone 0752 822236)

⓫ PAUL CORIN MUSICAL COLLECTION

This unusual collection of mechanical musical instruments includes fairground organs, pianos and street organs from all over Europe. Most of the exhibits can be heard every day. (Open May–Sept daily. ♿. 0579 43108)

⓬ POLPERRO

Polperro is one of the most picturesque of Cornwall's fishing villages. Many of its slate cottages, built into the hillside, have traditional outside steps. A fine example is the Shell House with its unusual shell-decorated exterior. Polperro was once notorious as a smuggling centre, aptly commemorated in the Smuggler's Museum. (Open Easter–mid Oct daily. ♿. Phone 0884 860847) No cars are allowed in the village centre so be prepared for walking. Look out for the Land of Legend and Model Village with its animated models that tell the story of the village. (Open Easter–Oct. ♿ ♿. Phone 0503 72378)

⓭ ST GERMANS

Cornwall's capital until 1043, this village is now a boating centre. The Augustinian priory here, St Germanus, is a fine example of Norman architecture. Nearby is Port Eliot, home to the Eliot family for over 400 years. The gardens (not open) were landscaped by Humphrey Repton in 1794. Also of interest are the restored gabled almshouses (1538) – the gables rest on stone columns forming a balcony with a separate outside flight of steps.

⓮ SALTASH

Charming hillside cottages and inns make Saltash well worth visiting. Fruit growing is important in the area around Saltash and in early summer the wooded slopes are ablaze with cherry blossom.

Preceding page: **St Michael's Mount** (JH)

Gorsedd 'Sword of Arthur' ceremony (AB)

Tin miners, Geevor (AB)

Geevor tin mine (AB)   **Granite wall** (JH)

Merry Maidens, St Buryan (AB)

The West Country has a richer tradition of myths and legends than any other part of England. The Celts may be responsible for this legacy. They lived here for centuries and were inveterate story-tellers and myth-makers. It's conceivable, too, that later generations dreamed up a few of the tales to make sense of some of the oddities in their world, such as stone circles, dolmens and standing stones. Each year a Celtic festival, the Cornish *Gorsedd*, is held at one of these sites, during which the 'Sword of Arthur' is drawn from a stone. We still don't know for sure where these stones came from or their true purpose. The most recent theory is that they were

Bedruthan Steps (AB)

ancient astronomical observatories used to track the moon and other celestial bodies. Our ancestors had a variety of different explanations. The stones at Men-an-Tol, for example, were thought by some to have healing powers; and by others, perhaps by those of a more pessimistic disposition, to be human beings turned to stone for their sins. The stones making up a circle cannot always be counted accurately. The Merry Maidens at St Buryan in Cornwall, for example, can only be counted by a woman, not by a man. These stones are also said to dance on Sundays!

Among the most famous legends of the West Country are those concerning the Giants. Historians believe that these stories may have been the Cornish people's response to a series of invasions by taller races, notably the Anglo-Saxons, Danes and Normans. No one today believes that Bedruthan Steps were really formed by the footsteps of a giant. But who can explain the discovery of a coffin measuring 11 feet (3 m) and containing a 2½-inch (6 cm) tooth? These items were unearthed at Tregony in the 17th century.

Tales of giants are especially numerous in West Cornwall. St Michael's Mount, near Penzance, is said to have been built by the giant Cormoran or, to be more accurate, his wife Cormelian. He delegated to her the task of carrying the massive blocks of granite from Penwith Moors to the building site. This left him free to doze in the sun. After the umpteenth journey, her knees and leather apron buckling under the weight of the rock, Cormelian decided to reduce her workload by using some nearby greenstone instead of the grey granite. Unfortunately for her, Cormoran was not colour blind as well as lazy. Waking briefly to check his wife's progress, he immediately spotted the deception. Enraged, he gave her a mighty kick which sent the greenstone flying into the sea. This piece of rock later surfaced just short of the Mount and is called Chapel Rock.

The piskies or Little People have also inspired their own folklore in most parts of Cornwall. There are many stories of people being enchanted, or 'piskie-led': being led a dance over the moors, unable to find their way back in the darkness, or wandering round a field and not being able to find the gate. These may sound like stories put about by habitual drunks. However, near Truro, a young boy was 'abducted' by the piskies and told how he had been taken to a fairy palace, fed with fairy food, and returned unharmed to his family some weeks later. Like his Irish counterpart, the leprechaun, the pisky was considered lucky, and to have one in the home will always bring good fortune.

Another group of spirits, called 'knockers' or 'nuggies', could be most unlucky and very spiteful if crossed. These small, withered creatures with large, ugly faces were believed to inhabit the tin mines. The miners went to some lengths to placate them. It was customary for the men to leave a crust or morsel of food. Swearing or whistling underground was likely to cause offence and considered very unlucky.

Plymouth, Dartmouth & S. Hams

Totnes (JH)

Salmon fisherman's cottage, Bantham (AB)

***Preceding page:** Bigbury Bay looking towards Burgh Island* (AB)

evon has a long and illustrious seafaring past. The 16th century saw the emergence of some of the most famous Devon nautical names – the Gilberts and the Grenvilles, and, of course, Sir Walter Raleigh and Sir Francis Drake. Plymouth, Devon's largest city, was the scene of one of the most famous episodes in British maritime history: the defeat of the Spanish Armada in 1588. All the local ports played their part by helping to build the ships that defeated the Spaniards, but Plymouth was chosen as the base port for the English fleet. Sir Francis Drake, the architect of Spain's defeat, moored his ships in the mouth of the River Plym, at Cattewater, south-east of the city. The Spanish fleet was first sighted in Devon from the cliffs near Hope Cove. The battle itself was fought at various points in the English Channel. Shortly before the battle Drake coolly played his famous game of bowls on Plymouth Hoe, one of the two natural features

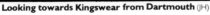

Looking towards Kingswear from Dartmouth (JH)

Francis Drake Memorial, Plymouth (AB)

Blackpool Sands, near Dartmouth (AB)

(the other is Plymouth Sound) that make Plymouth a stunning cityscape. A statue of Sir Francis stands on the Hoe, alongside Smeaton's Tower, the re-erected base of the old Eddystone Lighthouse.

Drake's naval exploits are part of Plymouth's heritage and it is for these that he is best remembered. His effect on the city, though, found expression in other ways. Drake, for example, built a freshwater leat, or waterway, from Dartmoor into the city. Much of this system remains today on the moor and in the city and urban areas.

Plymouth is still an extremely important naval base, making use of the spectacular natural harbour which is Plymouth Sound and of the rivers that flow into it. It is also a major car, passenger and freight port, linking to France and Spain.

The city was virtually flattened by bombs during World War II. What wasn't devastated at this time was later removed as part of the post-War rebuilding programme. The renewal of the city   63

Dartmouth (WCTB)

Kingsbridge harbour (AB)

East Portlemouth, (AB)

Dartmouth Castle (WCTB)

centre, under the Abercrombie plan, has resulted in wide pedestrianized streets and modern architecture. However, there is still an old quarter, the Barbican, with its narrow, cobble-stoned streets, timber-framed houses and fish market.

The Pilgrim Fathers sailed from Plymouth to the New World in 1620. The American connection with the city remains strong; many of the modern industries investing in the city are American. The city's international reputation is further maintained by its importance as a yachting centre. Each year Plymouth is host to a variety of transatlantic, even global, sailing events.

Devonport was absorbed by Plymouth after the establishment of the dockyard at Hamoaze in 1691 and became the city's naval quarter. The Town Hall, Gun Wharf (1718) and the Royal Naval Hospital are Devonport's most notable sites. Just off Devonport, in Plymouth Sound, is Drake's Island (formerly St Nicholas's Island) which was renamed in honour of Sir Francis Drake when he was made governor of the island and began to fortify it. The island was used as a prison in the 17th century, and is now used as an adventure centre where young people are trained in sailing, canoeing and climbing. The island is open to the public in the summer.

The lush green countryside of the South Hams lies within an area bounded by Dartmoor to the north, the rivers Yealm and Dart to the west and east respectively and the coast to the south. It is well worth exploring. The landscape has been shaped by the rivers that drain off Dartmoor — such as the Avon and the Dart — and culminate in deepwater creeks. These fjord-like formations give the South Hams its special character. Exploring the area by car is difficult. There are few bridges, so you will constantly find yourself doubling back along the river valleys. One of the best ways to explore the coastline is on foot. The coastline of this part of Devon has been saved from over-development thanks to the concerted efforts of the local authorities, the Countryside Commission and the National Trust. Under the Trust's Enterprise Neptune programme, for example, 35 miles (56 km) of coastline, beginning at Wembury near Plymouth, have been acquired.

The Great Mewstone Rock in Wembury Bay has twice been used as a place of imprisonment. Burgh Island, off Bigbury-on-Sea, offers a different kind of accommodation. The luxury Art Deco-style hotel built here in 1929 by wacky millionaire

Royal Albert (left) and Tamar bridges (WCTB)

Warehouse doors, Plymouth (JH)

Outside Totnes (JH)

Archie Nettlefold to entertain his friends and business associates has long been a haunt of the rich and famous: Noel Coward stayed here, as did the Duke of Windsor and Mrs Simpson, and later on, the Beatles. Agatha Christie wrote six of her books here, and used the island itself as a setting for her novel, *Evil Under The Sun*. If your budget won't allow you to stay at the hotel, head for the Pilchard Inn, the sole surviving building of the 14th-century settlement that used to be here. The inn is said to be haunted by the ghost of a smuggler. One of the county's most famous products, clotted cream, originated in South Devon. It fully justifies its reputation as the richest, most fattening and delicious cream in the world. Unlike the rest of us, Devonians don't regard

66

Dartington Hall (WCTB)

The Hoe, Plymouth (AB)

Salcombe (WCTB)

clotted cream as a treat, and cream teas, with scones and jam, are simply part of everyday living. Clotted cream is made by heating the cream slowly for a long time, and then skimming off the surface crust after the cream has cooled. Devon has always been renowned for its good food, and especially its mackerel, fresh crabs, farmhouse cheese and butter, salmon and trout. Traditional drinks include local cider or the deceptively lethal 'scrumpy', beer, mead and, more recently, wine. Although the Devon wine industry is still in its infancy, local winegrowers have already produced several prizewinning vintages. Devon wine is predominantly light, flowery and fresh-tasting, made from German grapes which can survive Britain's changeable weather.

❶ BIGBURY-ON-SEA

This is a very attractive and popular spot. You reach Burgh Island from here, at high tide via the sea-tractor, an odd-looking vessel which safely navigates the 7 or so feet of water, and at low tide by simply walking across the sands.

❷ DARTINGTON

The gardens of 14th-century Dartington Hall are open to the public all year round and the Hall itself (now an art college) only at certain times. A number of events are held here in summer (Phone 0803 862271).

Nearby is the Dartington Cider Press Centre, where a group of shops sell handmade products, including toys, rugs, clothes and glass. Also here is a riverside trail and picnic area. Refreshments. (Open all year, Mon–Sat; end July–early Sept, Sun too. Phone 0803 862367)

❸ DARTMOOR WILDLIFE PARK

An unusual zoo which, by the use of clever landscaping, allows you to see the more friendly species at close quarters. (Open all year daily. Phone 0755 37209)

❹ DARTMOUTH

The town's maritime history is well documented in the museum (Butter-walk); the collection of ship models is first rate. The Naval College, on a hill overlooking the town, is only open one day a year. Dartmouth Castle (1481) was one of the first castles specially built for artillery. A chain was slung from here to neighbouring Kingswear Castle to defend the castle in times of war. (Open Apr–Sept daily; Oct–Mar, Tues–Sun) At Dartmouth Pottery you can watch china ornaments being made. (Open Easter–Dec daily; Jan–Mar, Mon–Fri) ✆ 0803 834224

❺ HALLSANDS

The site of the Hallsands disaster, where a row of 37 houses collapsed in a storm in 1917 after the excavation of 500,000 tons of shingle offshore had removed the houses' natural barrier against the elements. A few of the devastated houses are still standing.

❻ INNER HOPE

One of the many unspoilt villages left in Devon. It is noted for its beautiful square of thatched cottages.

❼ KINGSBRIDGE

This market town is well worth exploring. The 16th-century Shambles with its old market building is perhaps the most outstanding structure but also visit Fore Street with its curious passages and alleys. The Cookworthy Museum gives the history of rural life in Devon and includes reconstructions of a farmhouse kitchen, scullery and dairy. (Open Easter–Sept, Mon–Sat; Oct, Mon–Fri) At the bottom of the town is the Kingsbridge Miniature Railway which will take you on a fun trip along the estuary and quay. (Open Easter; mid May–mid Sept daily. ✆ Phone 062682 361) ✆ 0548 853235

❽ OVERBECKS

The scientist Otto Overbeck created a small private museum in his house. The museum contains shipbuilding tools, detailed models of ships and replicas of shipwrecked vessels. You can also see Overbeck's electric rejuvenator (said to inject new life into the weary!), natural history exhibits, a collection of rare butterflies and a 6-acre garden. (Open April–Oct daily. Phone 054884 2893)

❾ PLYMOUTH

The town during the days of the Spanish Armada can be re-lived at The Armada Experience (New Street, the Barbican). The 16th-century Merchant's House Museum charts all aspects of Plymouth's history up to 1670. (Open Easter–Sept, Mon–Sat and Sun afternoon; Oct–Mar, Mon–Sat) The Mayflower Stone (Sutton) marks the departure point of the Pilgrim Fathers (1620). Aboard HMS *Plymouth* (Millbay Docks) there's an exhibition of recent naval history.

The City Museum and Art Gallery includes collections of natural history, insects and plants, paintings, ceramics, glass, silver and costumes. (Open all year, Mon–Sat) ✆ 0752 264849

❿ PLYMPTON

An important town in the Middle Ages, Plympton has a Norman keep, two medieval churches and a 16th-century Guildhall. At Plym Valley Railway Steam Centre you can watch old engines and coaches being restored. Souvenir shop and refreshments. (Open all year, Sun only. ♿ Phone 0752 795905)

Just off the A38 (Plymouth direction) is Saltram House, originally Tudor but extensively redesigned in the 18th century; two rooms are by Robert Adam. Refreshments. (Open Apr–Oct, Sun–Thurs, Fri–Sat afternoons only ♿. Phone 0752 336546)

⓫ SALCOMBE

This former fishing centre, an important harbour for yachtsmen, is beautifully situated and has a mild climate. Well worth a visit but crowded in summer. ✆ 0548 843927

⓬ SLAPTON LEY

Britain's largest freshwater lagoon, now a nature reserve. Separated from the sea by a shingle bar – Slapton Sands – the beach was used as a training ground for the Normandy landings in World War II.

⓭ TOTNES

The town is dominated by its Norman castle. (Open all year daily except Tues and Wed mornings). The Elizabethan House Museum has a costume room, dolls' houses and furniture, craftsmen's tools and re-creations of a period kitchen and grocer's shop. (Open Apr–Oct, Mon–Fri and Bank Hols) Totnes Motor Museum (Steamer Quay) houses a collection of vintage, sports and racing cars; also engines, motorbikes, bicycles and toy cars. (Open Easter–Oct daily ♿) The Devonshire Collection of Period Costume (High Street) has examples of clothing from the mid 18th century to the present day. The Dart Valley Railway runs through lovely countryside between Totnes and Buckfastleigh, where you can see engines and coaches being repaired. (Trains run Jun–Aug daily; Apr–May and Sept–Oct, certain days. ♿ Phone 0364 42338) ✆ 0803 863168

The Devon Riviera

Dawlish (JH)

Torquay harbour (AB)

Cockington (WCTB)

Torbay, near Goodrington (JH)

Teignmouth (JH)

Preceding page: **Oddicombe Beach from Babbacombe** (JH)

Torbay is the most popular British holiday area after Blackpool. The three main resort towns that make up Torbay are Torquay, Paignton and Brixham. Visitors have flocked to this part of the Devon coast since the early 19th century, attracted by its palm trees, balmy climate and elegant architecture. A travel writer once remarked of Torquay, 'It is not England but a bit of sunny Italy taken bodily from its rugged coast and placed here amid the green lanes and the pleasant pastoral lands of beautiful Devon.' The equally well-travelled Napoleon Bonaparte is reputed to have remarked 'Quel bon pays' ('What

Teignmouth harbour (JH)

a beautiful country') on seeing this part of the Devon coast from the deck of the British warship *Bellerophon* before being taken to St Helena.

The town began to develop as a resort during the Napoleonic Wars when the leisured classes were forced to look away from the Continent and to their native land for places of amusement and interest to visit. The British navy played a major part in the area's development, too. Torbay was an anchorage for the Fleet during the war with France, and the officers would seek accommodation ashore for their wives and daughters. The pleasant situation of Torquay made it a natural choice and the first houses of any note in the town were built for these officers and their families. The beneficial effects of the mild climate and sea air were soon discovered and it wasn't long before doctors were recommending Torquay and the Torbay area as a good place for convalescents and consumptives. (Torquay's motto is, appropriately, *Salus et Felicitas* – Health and Happiness.) Many wealthy families moved to the area for health reasons. The sewing machine magnate Isaac Singer, for example, built a large house in Paignton, Oldway Mansion.

North of Torquay (JH)

Oldway Mansion, Paignton

Torquay harbour (JH)

One of the leading lights in Torquay's development as a resort was Sir Robert Palk, formerly governor of Madras. He had already amassed considerable wealth in India when he was bequeathed a second fortune by a friend, General Stinger Lawrence. This second fortune included land in the form of Tor Quay, which he then set about developing. On the heights around Hope's Nose, you can still sense the elegant ambience of Torquay's Regency past. By 1848 the railway had arrived, and by 1850 Torquay was being promoted as the 'Queen of Watering Places'.

One of the other major resorts on this Riviera coast is Brixham, which played a leading role in the development of Devon's fishing industry. Fishing on a small scale has taken place in the tiniest harbours and coves along the Devon coast for centuries, but large-scale fishing operations only began in the late 18th century, with the introduction of the beam trawl at Brixham. (The beam trawl is a fishing trawler with beams that hold the ends of the trawl net apart, increasing the

Newton Abbot (JH)

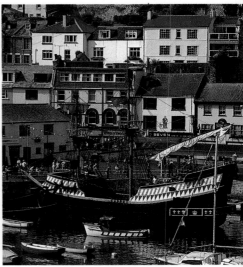

Brixham harbour (JH)

trawl area.) By 1851 Brixham had the largest fishery in England, supplying fresh fish to the markets of London, Bath and Bristol. The deep-sea industry effectively collapsed at the end of World War I. Local fishermen adapted as best they could and what remains of the industry is based on inshore fishing.

Visitors to the beautiful old village of Cockington, just outside Torquay, may marvel at the lovely old buildings and thatched cottages which are so much a part of Devon's rustic charm. In

recent years, however, it has been feared that some of the ancient skills, such as thatching, slating, cob wall-building and wheel making may die out unless a new generation of craftsmen emerges. The Devon Rural Skills Trust has been set up to encourage the training and practice of these ancient crafts. The trust, which is a registered charity, is based at Cockington Court. Here, you can have tea and cakes in elegant surroundings, watch craftsmen at work or stroll through the very attractive parkland.

75

❶ BERRY POMEROY

The ruined 14th-century Pomeroy Castle has a second building within its walls, a large country house built by the Seymour family. The house was later abandoned and allowed to fall down; no one knows why. The setting is picturesque, and there are pleasant walks to be enjoyed in the woods surrounding the castle. (Open all year daily)

❷ BRADLEY MANOR

This medieval manor-house is a mix of architectural details – a medieval layout, painted Tudor decorations and 17th-century plasterwork. (Open Apr–Sept, Wed afternoons only)

❸ BRIXHAM

This old fishing town is now the home of the British Fisheries Museum. (Open Jun–Sept daily; Oct–May, Tues–Fri, Mon afternoon and Sat morning) Outside Brixham is Berry Head. There's been a fort here since the Iron Age; a full history of the place is given at the visitors' centre. The area is also a nature reserve. The cliffs are a nesting place for kittiwakes, guillemots, kestrels and rock doves. Wonderful views over Torbay can be had from the lighthouse and lookout point. ☎ 08045 2861

❹ COCKINGTON

Cockington is a village within Torquay. It was originally an estate village built to serve nearby Cockington Court, a mansion set in 270 acres of parkland. (Open Easter–Oct daily) Most of the older houses were built around 1800, although there are some attractive, more recent buildings, such as Drum Inn (1934). There is an authentic forge where you can watch the Cockington village blacksmith at work.

❺ DAWLISH

A delightful Regency resort with impressive literary connections, Dawlish has remained small thanks to its hillside position which limited its development. Jane Austen and Charles Dickens both visited Dawlish, and the local museum commemorates these famous visitors. (Open May–Sept, Mon–Sat and Sun afternoon) In the town centre you'll find Dawlish Water, sometimes called the Brook, which runs through the Lawn, a miniature park complete with waterfalls and black swans. ☎ 0626 863589

❻ NEWTON ABBOT

A small racing town, Newton Abbot comes alive on market day (every Wed). In the woods behind Bradley Manor just outside the town centre (see above) there's a deep natural pit known as Puritan Pit. It was used by the nonconformists as a secret place of worship in the 17th century. Ford House (1610), now used by Teignbridge Council, has had many important visitors including Charles I and William of Orange. ☎ 0626 67494

❼ PAIGNTON

Torquay's sister resort; what Paignton lacks in architectural beauty it makes up for with superior sandy beaches, such as Goodrington Sands and Paignton Sands. Oldway Mansion (1874) should not be missed. Nicknamed 'The Wig-wam' by its builder, Isaac Singer, the house is, in fact, enormous, with a French-style neo-classical exterior and elegant interior. The gardens are equally as impressive. (Open all year, Mon–Fri) Paignton has the largest zoo in Devon, featuring many species of exotic birds and a landscaped ape house. (Open all year daily) Quaywest, an outdoor water theme park with water sports and fun boats is ideal for children. Refreshments. (Open May–Sept daily) Just outside Paignton you will find the 14th-century Compton Castle, now completely restored by the National Trust. (Open Apr–Oct, Wed–Fri and Sun)

Steam fans can take a trip on the Dart Valley Railway, which runs between Paignton and Kingswear. (Services run Spring Bank Hol–Sept daily; Oct, Sun and Thurs; other times, some Sundays. Phone 0803 555872 for info) ☎ 0803 558383

❽ POWDERHAM CASTLE

Originally built in medieval times as a fortified castle, Powderham Castle has been the home of the Courtenay family, the Earls of Devon, since 1390. It was extended in the 18th and 19th centuries. The park is regarded as one of the most beautiful in the country, with avenues of cedar trees and a herd of fallow deer. (Open Jun–mid Sept, Sun–Thurs afternoons only. Phone 0626 890243)

❾ SHALDON

An unspoilt coastal village with rows of terraced cottages. Shaldon has two beaches, one of which can be reached through a 'smugglers' tunnel'.

❿ TEIGNMOUTH

Teignmouth is divided into two distinct parts: the seafront with its grand 19th-century villas, and the warren of narrow, winding streets at the back of the town. Teignmouth is a centre for watersports. ☎ 0626 779769

⓫ TORQUAY

Pleasant vistas and numerous tourist attractions, ranging from crazy golf to coastal walks, are Torquay's alternatives to large sandy beaches. Marine Drive traverses the headland and offers superb views across the bay. On the clifftop above Anstey's Cove lies the ancient settlement of Kent's Cavern, which was inhabited as long ago as 30,000 BC; many of the finds from here are on display at Torquay Museum (Babbacombe Road). (Open Easter–Oct, Mon–Sat; Nov–Mar, Mon–Fri) The 12th-century Torre Abbey (Seafront) was converted into a private home after 1539 and later (18th century) remodelled as a mansion. The Abbey's present owners, Torquay Corporation, use part of the building as mayoral chambers and some of the rooms as an art gallery; several paintings by William Blake are in the collection. (Open Apr–Oct daily, mornings only; Nov–Mar by appointment) Babbacombe Model Village has miniature replicas of interesting houses and scenic landscapes in the area. Outdoor. (Open all year daily) At Oddicombe Beach you'll find a novel cliff railway which takes you down the steep drop to the shore (May–Oct only). ☎ 0803 214885

Dartmoor

DEVON AND CORNWALL

Preceding page: **Dartmoor**(JH)

Castle Drogo (JH)

Clapper bridge (JH)

Dartmoor ponies (AB)

View across Dartmoor (JH)

Tavistock Inn, Poundsgate (AB)

80

Visitors to Devon are accustomed to thinking of Dartmoor as one of the country's leading areas of natural beauty, but it is only during the past 150 years or so that it has been fully appreciated and not dismissed as a barren wasteland with a high rainfall.

Dartmoor occupies an area of 365 square miles (945 sq km) and in places rises to over 2000 feet (615 m). Geologically, Dartmoor is very different from Exmoor. It is made from plutonic rocks extruded at great temperatures over 250 million years ago. These granite foundations were later overlaid with sedimentary rocks, which in places have weathered to produce the famous Dartmoor tors ('tor' means 'high place'), huge pillars of rough granite rising up from the bracken on the hillsides. The southern edges of the moor are far more scenic than the grim-faced landscape towards the centre.

There is archaeological evidence that Dartmoor was well populated until the Iron Age, when the climate grew cooler and the hunter-gatherers moved to the lowlands. The moors are rich in well-preserved examples of prehistoric remains because the granite used by early man to build his dwellings was so durable. Ceremonial stone circles and hut circles can be seen all over the moor; the stone row which stretches from Stall Moor to Greenhill is thought to be longest in the world. There is evidence that people settled on the moor again during the Middle Ages; there are farm systems that date from this time around Postbridge, and at Hound Tor you can see an entire deserted medieval village.

Copper, lead, iron and especially tin were mined here from the 12th century until the early part of this century. Disused workings are a common sight. There are no working mines on Dartmoor apart from those used for china clay. Dartmoor granite is still quarried here; the granite for Nelson's Column and New Scotland Yard as well as the old London Bridge came from Dartmoor.

The 19th century saw the arrival of tourism, mainly in the form of painters, watercolourists and ramblers drawn to the place by its unorthodox natural beauty. The Dartmoor Preservation Association was set up in 1833 to fight an attempt by the Army to requisition the moor and use it as a firing range. The committee included the photographer Robert Burnard. (His granddaughter, Lady Sayer, 84, is the current head of the Association.) The Army partly won their case, and

Dartmoor Prison, Princetown (AB)

Drewsteignton (AB)

Widecombe-in-the-Moor (JH)

33,000 acres of north Dartmoor were given over to military use. The firing range is rarely used at weekends, but do be sure to keep an eye open for red warning flags if you are out walking in the area.

The long-standing custom of visitors to Dartmoor signing a book began in 1854. A Dartmoor guide, James Perrott, left a receptacle at Cranmere Pool in which visitors left their calling cards and signed a visitors' book. Later, when postcards were introduced, the custom began of stamping and self-addressing them for the next visitor to post in the official postbox. In this way the visitor could tell how quickly the next person visited that particular spot. Nowadays each Dartmoor letter-box has a visitors' book and rubber stamp and pad. The rubber stamp is used on the postcard, which is then put in the box by the first visitor to pick it up.

Dartmoor's famous prison is at Princetown. It was built between 1806 and 1809 to house prisoners captured during the Napoleonic Wars.

Okehampton Castle (WCTB)

Buckland-in-the-Moor (WCTB)

Prisoners were enlisted to build the parish church, which is a rather odd-looking edifice with four square pillars and very narrow aisles. In the graveyard you can see a tall granite prisoners' cross, a memorial to all the prisoners who have died here since 1900; the men are buried in unmarked graves. Princetown itself is a grim, forbidding place; perhaps the brightest spot is the local pub, The Plume of Feathers, a particularly welcoming hostelry with good beer and tasty food.

Dartmoor has its own special type of farmhouse, called the longhouse, which dates from the 15th century. Longhouses look similar to other farmhouses from the outside. Inside, though, they are unusual in that they are designed to house both people and animals under the same roof. Though this arrangement sounds primitive, it is very practical. Longhouses are a common sight in mainland Europe. In Britain, Dartmoor is the only place where evidence of them can still be found; at Hound Tor, for example.

Dartmoor's high rainfall has created many

Ashburton (JH)

permanently boggy areas, so take care if you are walking on the moors and be sure to wear stout shoes or walking boots. There are lichens, heathers and bog-cotton to be seen here, as well as the usual moorland carpet of bracken, gorse and whortle-berry. The vegetation is carefully managed by the National Park Authority to prevent any one species getting out of control and taking over. Bird-lovers will find golden plovers and dunlins, who breed in the boglands, as well as woodlarks, skylarks and pipits.

The famous Dartmoor ponies have lived here since the 10th century. The present ponies are not genuine pure bred Dartmoor ponies but the product of constant in-breeding between any small pony owned and allowed to run on the moor by commoners. The ponies are rounded up each autumn (this is known as 'The Drift') and any stallion colts plus any runt mares born the previous spring are sold at one of the various pony fairs; these are held in several towns, including Tavistock and Bovey Tracey. Tavistock is famous in the area for its annual Goose Fair, held on the second Wednesday in October. On this day the ancient, stannery town is taken up with goose and cattle sales, busy market stalls and a funfair.

Hay Tor rocks (AB)

Granite wall, Dartmoor (JH)

Two Bridges, Dartmoor (JH)

Spinster's Rock (JH)

Dartmoor is home to several species of cattle, including the hardy black and dun Galloways. Finally, there are the famous Dartmoor sheep. The white-faced varieties have largely been superceded by the hardier Cheviot and shaggy Blackface, whose long, thick coats allow them to withstand the harshness of the Dartmoor winter.

The National Park Authority has set up a network of information centres for visitors to Dartmoor, with branches at Tavistock, Oke-hampton, New Bridge, Postbridge, Steps Bridge and Princetown. All are good departure points for walking tours of the moor.

❶ ASHBURTON

Formerly a clothing centre and stannary town, Ashburton has a fine Gothic arch and several interesting old pubs.

❷ BOVEY TRACEY

The Devon Guild of Craftsmen show their wares in a converted granite mill on the River Bovey. Also in the village is Parke Rare Breeds' Farm, a private collection of horses, cattle, pigs, sheep and poultry. There is a pets' corner for children. The 200 acres of parkland offer many good walks. (Farm open Apr–Oct, daily; park open all year)

Whitestone Vineyards, near Bovey Tracey, is a working vineyard where you can watch English wine being made. ☎ 0626 832047

❸ BUCKFAST ABBEY

This famous abbey was founded in the 10th century. The monks of the Benedictine order who own the abbey make wine, cider and ornaments for sale to the public. (Open all year daily. Phone 0364 43301)

❹ BUCKLAND ABBEY

Built in 1278 by Cistercian monks, the house was bought in 1541 by the Grenville family. Sir Francis Drake acquired the property in 1581 and the exhibits are devoted to his exploits. Refreshments. (Open Apr–Oct, Fri–Weds; Nov–Mar, Wed, Sat and Sun afternoons only. Part ♿. Phone 0822 853607)

❺ BUCKLAND-IN-THE-MOOR

An unspoilt 'show' village which attracts thousands of visitors each year. The 15th-century St Peter's church has a beautiful rood screen and in the tower an unusual clock face on which the hours are marked by the letters 'My Dear Mother' instead of numerals.

❻ CASTLE DROGO

This fortress-like castle, designed by Sir Edward Lutyens, was probably the last great country house built in England. The huge granite structure looks positively medieval, but was actually commissioned by the self-made millionaire Julius Drewe in 1889. The castle has several very stylish sitting rooms and bathrooms as well as elaborate formal gardens. You enter the castle through a working portcullis which leads into a cathedral-like hall. There is a Wendy house to keep younger visitors amused. (Open Apr–Oct, Mon–Thurs, Sat–Sun)

❼ CHUDLEIGH

Only about a third of this medieval town was not destroyed by a great fire in 1807. On the site of the old Town Mills you'll find the Wheel Craft Centre where you can watch skilled craftsmen at work. Their products are for sale. (Open all year daily. Phone 0626 852698)

❽ DARTMEET

The East and West Dart rivers meet at this classic beauty spot.

❾ HAY TOR

This is one of is the most famous sites on Dartmoor. You get a wonderful view from the top.

❿ LYDFORD

At first glance, Lydford seems an undistinguished place, with an aspect more Cornish than Devonian. Its history is vastly more interesting than its looks. Lying between two deep valleys, the village has an excellent natural strategic position. King Alfred therefore chose it as one of his four defensive burghs in Devon in his war against the Danes. As a result, Lydford became an important local centre, with its own mint, and was the 'capital' of Dartmoor until it was superceded by Okehampton. The Castle (1195) and the nearby church of St Petrock are worth visiting.

Lydford is also the site of one of the most impressive natural features in Devon, the 1½-mile long, 200-foot (61.5 m) deep Lydford Gorge, shaped by the rushing waters of the River Lyd. The river produces spectacular effects at certain points along the thickly wooded Gorge, such as the churning at Devil's Cauldron or the 100-foot (30 m) White Lady waterfall, the highest on Dartmoor. (Open Apr–Oct daily; Nov–Apr daily, but from waterfall entrance as far as waterfall only)

⓫ MANATON

A pretty hamlet, once the home of the novelist John Galsworthy (of *Forsyte Saga* fame). Here you'll find a peaceful village green and a 15th-century church.

⓬ MEARSDON MANOR GALLERIES

Mearsdon Manor is a 13th-century mansion now used as galleries selling paintings, copper and bronze, carvings and jade.

⓭ MORWELLHAM QUAY

The historic installations at Morwellham, once a busy copper-loading port on the Tamar, have now been converted into an important industrial museum. (Open all year daily. Phone 0822 832766)

⓮ NORTH BOVEY

North Bovey is widely considered to be one of the most attractive villages in Devon. Near the village is the Miniature Pony Centre, where children can play with Shetland ponies and other miniature breeds. (Open Mar–Oct daily. ♿. Phone 0647 432400)

⓯ OKEHAMPTON

A pleasant market town situated very close to Dartmoor, Okehampton provides a good base for touring the area. The town's main attraction is the Norman Okehampton Castle, built by Baron Baldwin. The castle, now a ruin, stands on a narrow ridge just outside the town. (Open Apr–Sept daily; Oct–Mar, Tues–Sun) Okehampton Town Hall, built in 1685 as a private house, is also worth visiting. Opposite the Town Hall stands a Museum of Dartmoor Life, which records the day-to-day life of past generations of Dartmoor people. (Open all year, Mon–Sat and Sun in Jul–Aug) ☎ 0837 53020

⓰ WIDECOMBE-IN-THE-MOOR

The most famous village in Dartmoor has little to recommend it apart from its position, 800 feet (246 m) above sea level. You can get wonderful views from here. Widecombe Fair, immortalized in the song, is held on the second Tuesday in September.

Exeter & East Devon

Preceding page: **Sidmouth** (JH)

Tiverton church (JH)

Exmouth (JH)

Seafront, Sidmouth (JH)   **River Exe, Bickleigh**

Tiverton Castle (WCTB)

Exeter is the gateway to Devon and the county's administrative, commercial and cultural capital. It has been described as the most pleasant English city to live in. Exeter University campus is a good example of the care in planning that has maintained the city's attractiveness and its appeal. All over Exeter there are many little parks and oases of green where you can sit and watch the world go by. There are vantage points, too, giving views of the countryside.

Exeter (JH)

Exeter was inhabited by tribal Celts called the Dumnonii over two centuries before the Romans arrived and colonized the place. The Romans were quick to appreciate the advantages of Exeter's location, on a broad ridge of land which rises steeply from the left bank of the River Exe. They called the city 'Isca Damnoniorum' and promptly set about building walls around the city (parts of which can still be seen) and establishing a grid-like street pattern. The Romans also built a bath-house, which was discovered in 1970 beneath the cathedral, a market place and a basilica.

The city was later overrun by the Danes, and then rescued by King Alfred, who established a mint here. During the Norman conquest the city was besieged and eventually taken by William the Conqueror. Building of the Norman cathedral began soon after, but was not completed until the 14th century. The cathedral is noted for its 300-foot (90 m) nave and magnificent sculpted figures carved from local Beer stone. The remains of Rougemont Castle (named after the red colour of

Exeter Cathedral (JH)

Drake's Arms, Exeter (WCTB)

Looking west from Exmouth (JH)

Exeter wharf (JH)

the rock on which it was built) also date from this period. The Guildhall is said to be the oldest municipal building in Britain; there are references to it as far back as 1160. The exact date of building is not certain, but there are references to works in 1330 and we do know that it was added to in 1593. The Guildhall is roofed with gilded beams and carved figures of bears brandishing staves.

In medieval times the city's water distribution system consisted of a network of underground tunnels. You can still see the entrance to the

tunnels, in Princesshay. The cobbled medieval pathway that was formerly the main road into Exeter is still in evidence at Stepcote Hill.

Many parts of the city were destroyed during the last war, but the centre still has a remarkably high percentage of old buildings. The elegant Georgian terraces of Southernhay are just a stone's throw from the timber-framed shops and dwellings of Cathedral Close, which contains a mixture of architectual styles, from medieval to modern. The popular TV series 'The Onedin Line' was filmed in the old buildings of the Maritime Museum on the

92

Cathedral Close, Exeter (JH)

Exeter (JH)

quayside of the former port, on the south side of the city.

While Exeter is the principal town of Devon, one of the most beautiful must surely be Sidmouth. This town wasn't considered to be fashionable until Christmas Eve, 1819, when the Duke and Duchess of Kent arrived with their baby daughter, Princess Victoria, seeking refuge, some say, from the Duke's creditors. They stayed at Woolbrook Cottage, now the Royal Glen Hotel. Sidmouth became a society haunt overnight, patronized by the rich and famous. Elegant Regency and early

Victorian holiday homes were built in every available spot. Sidmouth became a centre for the 'cottage ornée', or rustic folly, inspired by Marie Antoinette's 'Le Petit Trianon' at Versailles. These strange-looking houses have elaborate thatched roofs, gothic windows and intricate tented verandahs and balconies with delicate ironwork, as you can see in the aptly named Elysian Fields.

Sidmouth is also famous for its Folklore Festival, held every August. The event, which covers music, song and dance from all over the world, is probably the biggest of its kind in the country. 93

❶ BEER

A pretty fishing village, renowned for its distinctive stone, quarried since Roman times. Explore the nearby caverns at Beer Quarry Caves (Open Easter–Oct daily. Phone 0297 20986/80282) Beer Heights Light Railway runs to the Pecorama Pleasure Gardens. Here there are model railways, gardens and adventure playgrounds. (Open Nov–Spring Bank Hol, Mon–Sat; Spring Bank Hol–Oct, daily. ⑇ ⚓ Phone 0297 21542)

❷ BICKLEIGH

Bickleigh, with its thatched cottages, river and many pubs, is a delight. Bickleigh Mill has a working watermill, exhibitions of farming methods and machinery and a trout fishery. (Open Easter–Christmas daily; Christmas–Easter weekends. ⑇ Phone 08845 419) Nearby Bickleigh Castle has a thatched Norman chapel, a vast gatehouse containing the Great Hall, and an armoury. There is a museum and garden. Refreshments. (Open Easter week; Spring Bank Hol–early Oct, Sun–Fri afternoons only. Phone 08845 363)

❸ BICTON PARK

These 60 acres of grounds contain one of Devon's finest gardens, laid out in 1735. There is an American garden and the Hermitage garden, which visitors are taken to on the Bicton woodland 18-inch (45 cm) gauge railway. Younger visitors will enjoy the space station replica. The museum has displays of old machinery, magic lantern shows and penny-slot machines. Refreshments. (Open mid Apr–Sept daily. Phone 0395 68465)

❹ BRANSCOMBE

Branscombe is known as one of the two 'longest villages' in England as well as one of the prettiest. St Winifred's Church has a Norman tower, three-tier pulpit, box pews and Elizabethan gallery. The local inn, The Mason's Arms, dates back 700 years.

❺ BUDLEIGH SALTERTON

This peaceful, seaside town is ideal for those who want to get away from it all. The Fairlynch Arts Centre and Museum has some fun exhibitions, including a smuggler's cellar. (Open Apr–Oct daily)

❻ EXETER

Among the city's many impressive buildings are the Norman Cathedral and the Guildhall (High Street). Exeter has three major museums. The Royal Albert Memorial Museum (Queen Street) has exhibits of natural and local history, archaeology and several fine art galleries. (Open all year, Tues–Sat. Closed Bank Hols) The Rougemont Museum (Castle Street) specializes in costume and lace. (Open all year daily) The Maritime Museum (The Quay) has over 130 vessels on display. (Open all year daily) ⧉ 0392 72434

❼ EXMOUTH

Sandy beaches make Exmouth a popular resort. Places to visit in the town include the Barn Hotel (1896/7), which was designed in a butterfly-shape. It is remarkable for its two huge round stone chimneys. The Wonderful World of Miniature is found on the seafront and has the largest 'OO gauge' model railway in the world. (Open Easter–Oct daily; Nov–Easter, Sat and Sun. ⚓) ⧉ 0395 263744

Two miles north of Exmouth stands A La Ronde (1795), an extraordinary 16-sided house which has remained virtually unchanged, inside and out. (Open Easter; Jun–Sept, Mon–Thurs. ⑇. Phone 0395 265514)

❽ HONITON

Honiton's pride is its lacemaking, a craft introduced by Flemish refugees over 200 years ago. The medieval chapel of Allhallows now houses the Allhallows Museum, which has Honiton lace on display and lacemaking demonstrations. (Open mid May–Oct, Mon–Sat) Just outside the town is Hembury Hillfort, Devon's best example of an earthwork. The Honiton Pottery is an important local attraction. (Factory open all year, Mon–Fri. Shop open daily) ⧉ 0404 43716

❾ KILLERTON

The hillside gardens of 18th-century Killerton House are especially lovely. The contents of the house include the Paulise de Bush collection of costume. Refreshments. (House open Apr–Oct, Wed–Mon; Grounds open all year daily ⑇. Phone 0392 881345)

❿ NEWTON POPPLEFORD

The café in this picturesque village is reputed to serve the best cream tea in Devon.

⓫ OTTERTON MILL CENTRE

A working watermill, with adjacent craft workshops, and arts and crafts exhibitions. (Open Easter–Oct daily; Nov–Easter weekends. Phone 0395 68521)

⓬ OTTERY ST MARY

Ottery St Mary is notable for the 13th-century Church of St Mary, which resembles a mini version of Exeter Cathedral. There are also some beautiful Georgian houses. ⧉ 0404 813964

⓭ SEATON

Once an important river port, Seaton turned to another form of transport when its channel became impassable. The famous Seaton Tramway operates open-top tram-cars in fine weather along the estuary to Colyton.

⓮ SIDMOUTH

This popular resort has many fine Regency buildings. Two miles from the town is the Donkey Sanctuary where 500 donkeys are cared for. (Open all year daily. ⚓ Phone 0395 578222) ⧉ 0395 516441

⓯ TIVERTON

Tiverton was famous as a wool-producing town in the 17th and 18th centuries. Tiverton Castle (1106) has an impressive medieval gatehouse and tower. Refreshments. (Open Good Friday–Sept, Sun–Thurs afternoons only) The Museum (St Andrew St) has excellent local history exhibits. (Open all year, Mon–Sat) ⧉ 0884 255827

Just outside Tiverton is Knightshayes Court (1870s), noted for its rich interior and fabulous formal garden. Refreshments. (Open Apr–Oct, Sun–Thurs, afternoons only ⑇. Phone 0884 254665)

North Devon

Coastline near Ilfracombe (WCTB)

Sign at entrance to Gammon Lane, Barnstaple (JH)

Preceding page: **Clovelly** (JH)

Ilfracombe harbour (AB)

Northern Devon is renowned for its unspoilt beauty and has comparatively few caravan parks, marinas and tourist shops. There has been little scope for development because most of the coastal area and the farmland adjacent to it belongs to the National Trust and a handful of landowning families. This is the ideal place for those who enjoy simple pursuits, such as walking or bird-spotting. You can happily combine the two here. The stretch of coastline between Ilfracombe, north Devon's leading resort, and Braunton Burrows, famous for its sand dunes, marsh and sea birds and plant life, is particularly rewarding.

From Torrs Park, a stone's throw west of Ilfracombe, the cliffs rise and fall for several miles, offering spectacular coastal scenery. At Lee you can either continue along the coast or opt for a change of scenery and take the path inland, through a valley of fuschias. The waters off the headland of Morte Point can be treacherous. This was reputedly a favourite place for wreckers during the 18th century. The wreckers would use lanterns to dupe unsuspecting merchantmen into thinking they were heading for Ilfracombe instead of a watery grave on the rocks. Lining Morte Bay is Woolacombe beach, one of the best in Devon

98

Croyde (AB)

Sweet's Cottage, Croyde (AB)

and a great favourite when the weather is fine.

Hartland Point is where the north-western frontier of Devon meets the full force of the Atlantic. Violent gales and mountainous seas are common here. The village of Hartland is situated several miles inland and yet still feels the effects of the Atlantic weather.

Peaceful and sheltered, Clovelly could not provide more of a contrast. It became an important fishing centre in the 16th century after George Cary, a local lawyer, built a stone pier, giving Clovelly the only safe harbour on the north coast between Appledore and Boscastle. Tourism re-

placed fishing as the main source of revenue late in the last century. The popularity of Clovelly was helped by the authors Charles Kingsley and Charles Dickens (in collaboration with Wilkie Collins) who described the town in their writings. (Charles Kingsley's father was rector of Clovelly in the 1830s.)

The town of Appledore, noted for its traditional skills in wooden boat-building, was also immortalized by Kingsley in *Westward Ho!* The success of the book prompted speculators to use the name for a new watering place they planned to build on a stretch of sand dunes near Appledore. Their

Torrington (WCTB)

Woody Bay (AB)

Bideford (JH)

Clovelly (JH)

Bideford (AB)

choice of site was not a fortunate one, however, given the ferocity of the Atlantic weather, and it wasn't long before the first buildings were washed away by the sea. Appledore has one of the few surviving shipyards in the area. Iron ships are produced here, in one of the biggest covered yards in Europe.

One of the most famous animals in literature was born in this part of Devon, between the rivers Taw and Torridge. Tarka (Celtic for 'little water wanderer') was immortalized by Henry Williamson in his book *Tarka the Otter*, first published in 1927. The film of the novel, made some 50 years later, was shot in the north Devon countryside. A 'Tarka Trail', an extensive linked system of walks through Tarka's hunting grounds, has been set up. The countryside hereabouts is

Cliffs at Hartland Quay (AB)

very attractive and varied, comprising woodland, pasture, river-valley and coast, and well promoted. British Rail, for example, have dubbed the Exeter–Barnstaple railway the 'Tarka Line'.

Another place of interest connected with wild-life is Lundy Island, situated 23 miles (37 km) west of Ilfracombe. The granite cliffs on Lundy rise vertically from the sea to around 500 feet (154 m) and attract a wide variety of bird life; over 400 different species of birds have been sighted here. The island itself is small – only 3½ miles long and half a mile wide – and has one hotel (Millcombe House), built in the 1830s, one pub and one church. The Marisco Tavern is named after Lundy's famous pirate, William de Marisco. Holiday accommodation on Lundy is limited, so booking well in advance is essential. Day trips to the island can be taken from Ilfracombe and Bideford.

❶ APPLEDORE

Appledore is a delightful old fishing village, built on a steep hillside. The little quayside lanes, or Opes, and the riverside cottages are charming. The Maritime Museum (Odun Street) has an exhibition devoted to nautical life. (Open Easter–Oct daily, Sat–Mon afternoon only. ♿. Phone 0237 474852)

❷ BAGGY POINT

These high sandstone cliffs form one of the two jutting headlands that surround Woolacombe, and form the basis of a lovely 2½-mile walk.

❸ BARNSTAPLE

Barnstaple is north Devon's principal town, and reputedly England's oldest borough. It became wealthy as a wool-producing town in the 18th century when many of its beautiful Georgian houses were built. The impressive Queen Anne's Walk (1708) by the river was the original trading exchange and is the town's most impressive building. Barnstaple has been famous for its pottery since medieval times and you can still see Royal Barum Ware being made at the factory in Barnstaple. Shop and restaurant. (Open all year, Mon–Sat; Jul–Aug, daily) St Anne's Chapel Museum (Church Lane) has a variety of objects dealing with Barnstaple's history, as well as having an interesting history itself. (Open Spring Bank Hol–Sept, Mon–Sat) ☎ 0271 47177

❹ BIDEFORD

Bideford is considered to be the most attractive town in north Devon. Its history lies in seafaring and shipbuilding, which was developed by the Grenville family in the 1740s. The collapse of the woollen industry destroyed Bideford's export trade, restricting commerce to coastal traffic. The town is built overlooking the quay, which bustles with fishing boats, cruisers and pleasure craft. There are some fine 17th-century former merchants' houses in Bridgeland Street. The Burton Art Gallery (Kingsley Road) has a permanent collection of paintings by English artists as well as model ships, German and English pottery and porcelain. (Open all year, Mon–Fri and Sat morning. Phone 0237 476713)

❺ BRAUNTON BURROWS

Braunton Burrows is one of the largest protected areas of sand dunes in the country – over 1000 acres of unspoilt terrain, wildflowers and wildlife. The Burrows run into Saunton Sands, a huge area of sand that is exposed at low tide.

❻ CLOVELLY

Clovelly really is a unique fishing village. There is only one main cobbled street, and this zig-zags down 400 feet (142 m) to the quay. For this reason no cars are allowed in the village, although a Land Rover service takes visitors to and from the Red Lion Inn on the quayside.

❼ CROYDE

This hilltop village has one of the best family beaches in Devon. On the edge of the village you'll find the Gem, Rock and Shell Museum, which contains a unique collection of local gemstones and shells. You can see demonstrations of gem cutting and polishing in the workshop. (Open mid Apr–Sept daily. Phone 0271 890407)

❽ GREAT TORRINGTON

The church at Great Torrington was the scene of the death of 200 Royalist soldiers in 1646. The Cromwellian forces had used the church as a gunpowder store as well as a prison and tragically the Royalist soldiers were blown up. A mound in the churchyard may well be the mass grave of the soldiers who died in the accident. The town is also the home of Dartington Crystal. There is a shop and you can watch glass being blown at the factory. Restaurant (Shop open all year, Mon–Sat. Factory open all year, Mon–Fri. Phone 0805 23797)

A mile south-east of the town you'll find Rosemoor Gardens, where you can see a superb display of rhododendrons, roses and ornamental trees and shrubs. (Open all year. Phone 0805 24067)

❾ ILFRACOMBE

North Devon's premier holiday resort, Ilfracombe became popular when the railway arrived here in 1874. Although tourism has recently declined due to competition from self-catering resorts, Ilfracombe still has many hotels and guest-houses, and a steady stream of pleasure boats operate between the resort and Bristol, Minehead, Lundy and Clovelly. Ilfracombe's location in a sheltered basin has restricted its expansion, although newer buildings straddle the hillsides leading out of the town. One of the town's oldest buildings is St Nicholas's Chapel, built above the harbour in the early 1300s as a waymarker and chapel for fishermen and sailors. There are plenty of amenities such as an indoor swimming pool, a golf course and theatre. The local museum (Wilder Road) has a varied display of exotic exhibits donated by former residents of the town. (Open Easter–Oct daily; Nov–Easter, Mon–Sat mornings. Phone 0271 863541)

A mile outside the town stands Chambercombe Manor, a medley of charming 16th- and 17th-century buildings built round a cobbled courtyard, with some fine furniture and a miniature chapel measuring only 10 feet (3 m) in length. (Open Easter–Sept, Mon–Fri and Sun afternoon. Phone 0271 862624)

❿ LUNDY

Lundy's history is strewn with tales of pirates – the Marisco Tavern is named after its most famous pirate, William de Marisco. Present-day Lundy Island is a haven for bird-watchers, with puffins being the main attraction.

⓫ MORTEHOE

Built largely of locally quarried Morte slate, Mortehoe lies in a blustery spot frequently battered by westerly gales. The Church of St Mary's has 16th-century bench ends carved with sea monsters, portraits and coats of arms.

⓬ WOOLACOMBE BEACH

With over 3 miles (5 km) of golden sand, this is one of north Devon's most famous beaches.

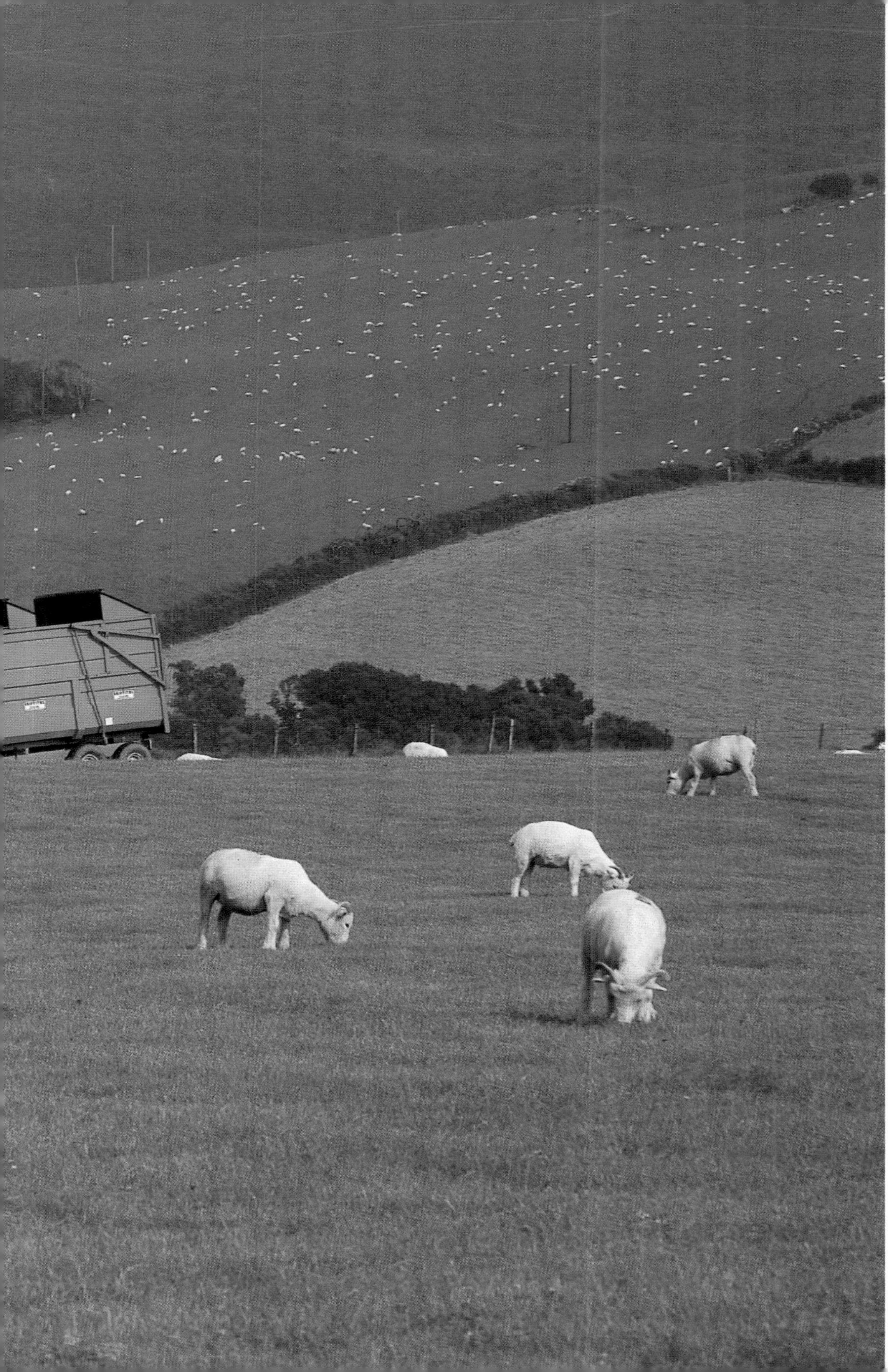

Exmoor & Central Devon

Preceding page:
Exmoor (JH)

Red deer stag, Exmoor (AB)

Valley of the Rocks, Lynton (AB)

Arlington Court (AB)

Although Somerset is the county that claims the greater part of Exmoor, several of its finest beauty spots fall within Devon's border. The moorlands are formed from layers of sedimentary rocks, sandstone, slate and limestone. Exmoor covers an area of 265 square miles (684 sq km). Its landscape is varied. On the bleak, windy hilltops the only cover is a scrubby, coarse layer of grass, bracken, heather and gorse. In the sheltered valleys the slopes are lush and wooded, with streams and waterfalls cascading down the hillsides on their way to the sea.

The picturesque village of Combe Martin is situated in one of these sheltered valleys. The climate is mild here and ideal for growing spring flowers and early fruit and vegetables. Strawberries from Combe Martin are often among the first to appear each year. The village is the home of one of the most interesting buildings in Devon, known as the Pack of Cards Inn. It's said that the house, which looks like a stack of cards, was built in the 18th century to celebrate a spectacular win at cards. The odd layout mirrors the numerical structure of a pack of cards: there are four floors, each

Hunter's Inn (AB)

Combe Martin (WCTB)

Heddon's Mouth (AB)

with 13 doors, and a total of 52 windows.

Much of the seaward edge of Exmoor is owned by the National Trust and is best explored on foot. You can spend an enjoyable day walking part of the Somerset–North Devon Coast Path, which extends from Minehead to Braunton Burrows. Just east of Combe Martin are the Little Hangman and the Great Hangman, two 'mini-mountains' which offer superb views of the coastline. East of here is Heddon's Mouth with its steep valley covered in sandstone scree, known as Hangman grit. The path then leads through one of the finest

parts of the north Devon coast to the aptly named Woody Bay.

Many people visit the northern part of Exmoor because of its associations with the Doones, a notorious family of outlaws who, according to legend and R.D. Blackmore's novel, *Lorna Doone*, terrorized Exmoor during the 17th century. During the holiday season a small bus runs from Lynton to the pretty village of Malmsmead, just over the border in Somerset, and then on to various points of interest along the valley of Badgworthy Water (May–end Oct twice daily. Phone 0598 52470).

Badgworthy Water (AB)

Lynmouth (WCTB)

Lorna Doone farm, Malmsmead (AB)

You can also walk the Doone trail. A footpath from Malmsmead leads to the combe called Doone Valley. Nearby is Hoccombe Combe and the ruins of houses said to have been occupied by the Doones.

The most recent Exmoor legend concerns the Beast. (Dartmoor allegedly has one of these too.) Many people in the area believe that some big cat, or cats, roams the moor. The evidence is dead and half-eaten sheep which, they say, have been killed in a way quite untypical of a savage dog. There have been several sightings, too, of large cat-like creatures.

Exmoor is rich in minerals and especially iron, which was mined from the 13th century until the end of the 19th century with a brief resurgence during World War I. Copper, manganese, silver and even gold have been extracted from here.

The burial grounds of Chapman Burrows are evidence that early man settled on Exmoor in relatively large numbers. On the outer rim of the moor is Shoulsbarrow Castle, a large Iron-Age hill fort reached via a 'permissive' footpath; the fort is on private land through which there is no public right of way. The fort covers several acres and can be bewildering at first. The very regular shape of

Crediton church (JH)

Watersmeet (AB)

Exmoor (JH)

the fort suggests Roman influence. The Romans did not settle on Exmoor but one theory is that they used the fort as a kind of tax office, where the local people came to pay their dues.

Like Dartmoor, Exmoor is famous for its wild ponies. These are believed to be directly descended from the wild horses of the Iron Age. The two breeds are different. In Exmoor it is still possible to find herds of pure-bred ponies running wild.

The deer on Exmoor, like other wild animals, belong to whoever owns the land on which they are found. Ownership can therefore change hands several times in one day!

❶ ARLINGTON COURT

This is a house of contrasts, for the rather forbidding exterior of Arlington Court gives no clue to the riot of Victorian clutter within. The house was created for the Chichester family by a local architect, but its weird and wonderful decor is totally the invention of Miss Rosalie Chichester, a great eccentric, who lived here for 84 years until she died in 1949. She was an avid traveller, and the house is full of mementoes of her world voyages, including model ships, Pacific shells, birds, butterflies and trinkets, a red amber elephant from China, and innumerable watercolours of her favourite scenes.

A great animal lover, Miss Chichester also established a wildlife refuge at Arlington, and you can still see Jacob sheep and Shetland ponies wandering around the landscaped grounds! There is a small formal garden and a beautiful old conservatory overlooking three grassy terraces and a fountain pool. Restaurant. (House open Apr–Oct, Sun–Fri and Sat Bank Hols; Park open all year daily. ♿. Phone 0271 850296)

❷ CHITTLEHAMPTON

Deep in the heart of rural Devon lies this old Saxon settlement, surrounded by rolling, patchworked hills and pastures, and enjoying a delightfully sheltered position. Chittlehampton's church of St Urith which has the finest tower (114 ft/40.5 m) in Devon, is flanked by the Square or town meeting-place. St Urith or Hieritha was a Saxon saint who was murdered by the savage folk of Chittlehampton, who hacked her to pieces with their scythes. Inside the church, you can see a 15th-century pulpit intricately carved with likenesses of five saints, including St Urith. The tower is exquisitely decorated, and it's easy to see how the local saying originated: 'Bishop's Nympton for length, South Molton for strength and Chittlehampton for beauty'.

At nearby Cobbaton, there's a Combat Vehicles Museum with a good collection of vehicles from World War II. There is also a shop and a children's adventure play-ground. (Open Apr–Oct daily. ♿ ⛴. Phone 07694 414)

❸ COMBE MARTIN

Between the 13th and late 19th centuries, Combe Martin was an important centre for tin and silver mining. However, there are very few remains of these industries. The most intriguing sight in the village is the 18th-century Pack of Cards Inn. Other places of interest include the Combe Martin Motor-cycle Collection (Cross Street). The museum takes a nostalgic look at British bikes and other paraphernalia, including petrol pumps and garage signs. (Open Easter; mid May–mid Sept daily. ⛴. Phone 027188 2346) Also well worth visiting is the Higher Leigh Manor Wildlife and Leisure Park. Set in 20 acres of wooded valley the park has an amazing range of rare animals including otters, meerkats and various species of monkey. The park itself has been planted with rare species of trees, shrubs and bushes; the Japanese Garden is in the process of being restored. There is an adventure playground and animal handling sessions. (Open Easter–Oct daily; Nov–Easter, Sat and Sun. ⛴. Phone 027188 2486)

❹ EXMOOR BIRD GARDENS

A haven for bird-lovers, the Bird Gardens are set in 12 acres of landscaped gardens. Here you can see a wide range of ornithological species, including tropical and exotic birds, waterfowl and penguins. There's also a 'Tarzanland' play area for children. (Open all year daily. ⛴. Phone 05983 352)

❺ LYNTON AND LYNMOUTH

These sister villages became popular holiday resorts over a century ago. Lynton sits on the hilltop, while Lynmouth basks on the seashore 600 feet (200 m) below. The two villages are linked by a zig-zag road and the intriguing cliff railway, opened in 1890 as the gift of print tycoon Sir George Newnes. The two villages are very different in character: Lynton is a small town rather than a village, and although by no means as beautiful as some traditional Devon villages it has some pleasant weatherboarded houses. The Lyn and Exmoor Museum is found in the pretty St Vincent's Cottage. Here you'll find exhibits on traditional Exmoor life. (Open Apr–Sept, Mon–Fri and Sun afternoon) ☎ 0598 52225

Lynmouth occupies a scenic position at the junction of the East and West Lyn rivers, which Gainsborough considered the 'most delightful place for a landscape painter this country can boast'. Sadly, Lynmouth is best known in modern times for the disastrous floods that devastated the village in 1952, wrecking the community and resulting in 34 deaths. Strong new flood barriers were built and both Lyn rivers were widened to prevent such a tragedy ever happening again.

❻ MARTINHOE

Situated on the east side of the spectacular Heddon Valley, Martinhoe is a tiny remote parish with an attractive church. A mile north-east of the village is Woody Bay. The cliffs here offer some of the most breathtaking views in north Devon.

❼ SOUTH MOLTON

This pretty town lies just south of Exmoor, and was a prosperous wool town in the Middle Ages. An elegant Georgian square, Guildhall and Assembly Rooms tell of the town's former wealth. Today, it is a busy agricultural centre. Well worth a visit is Quince Honey Farm. (Open all year daily. Phone 07695 2401)

❽ TRENTISHOE

Trentishoe is the twin village of Martinhoe and equally as remote. It too has a parish church of interest. Nearby Hunter's Inn is very popular with walkers. It has all-round outstanding views.

❾ WATERSMEET

Watersmeet is the meeting-point of the East Lyn River and Hoar Oak Water, and is one of the classic beauty spots of north Devon. Watersmeet House, a fishing lodge built in 1832, is now a National Trust information centre. Refreshments. (Open Apr–Oct daily. Phone 0598 53348)

Page numbers in italics indicate a gazetteer entry